D0467949

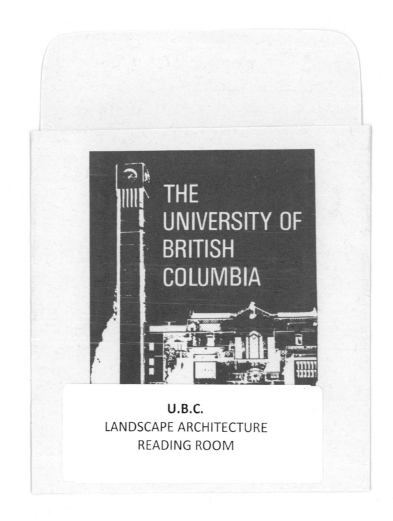

THE
UNIVERSITY OF
BRITISH
COLUMBIA

THE
CLASSICAL
GARDENS
OF CHINA

THE CLASSICAL GARDENS OF CHINA

HISTORY AND DESIGN TECHNIQUES

YANG HONGXUN

TRANSLATED BY
WANG HUI MIN

Photographs by Wang Zheng Gui

 VAN NOSTRAND REINHOLD COMPANY
NEW YORK CINCINNATI TORONTO LONDON MELBOURNE

Library of Congress Catalog Card Number 81-23974

ISBN 0-442-23209-8

Printed in the United States of America

Designed by Iris Weinstein

Published by Van Nostrand Reinhold Company Inc.
135 West 50th Street
New York, NY 10020

Van Nostrand Reinhold Publishers
1410 Birchmount Road
Scarborough, Ontario M1P 2E7, Canada

Van Nostrand Reinhold Australia Pty. Ltd.
480 Latrobe Street
Melbourne, Victoria 3000, Australia

Van Nostrand Reinhold Company Limited
Molly Millars Lane
Wokingham, Berkshire, England

16 15 14 13 12 11 10 9 8 7 6 5 4 3 2 1

Frontispiece: A scene of the Wang Chuan Garden, originally drawn by Wang Wei, famous painter and poet of the Tang dynasty and owner of the garden. This copy was made from a stone carving reproduction by Guo Shi Yuan of the Ming dynasty.

Library of Congress Cataloging in Publication Data

Yang, Hongxun.
    The classical gardens of China.

    Includes index.
    1. Gardens, Chinese. 2. Gardens—China—History.
3. Gardens, Japanese—Chinese influences. 4. Gardens, European—Chinese influences. I. Wang, Hui Min. II. Title.
SB457.55.Y3613   712′.0951   81-23974
ISBN 0-442-23209-8   AACR2

CONTENTS

CHRONOLOGY

Xia Dynasty (c. 2205–c. 1766 B.C.)
Shang Dynasty (c. 1766–c. 1122 B.C.)
Zhou Dynasty (c. 1122–249 B.C.)
    Western Zhou (c. 1122–771 B.C.)
    Eastern Zhou (770–249 B.C.)
    Spring and Autumn period (770–481 B.C.)
    Warring States period (403–221 B.C.)
Qin Dynasty (221–207 B.C.)
Han Dynasty (202 B.C.–A.D. 220)
    Former (Western) Han (202 B.C.–A.D. 9)
    Xin dynasty (A.D. 9–23)
    Later (Eastern) Han (A.D. 25–220)
Three Kingdoms
    Wei (220–265)
    Shu (221–265)
    Wu (222–280)
Jin Dynasty (265–420)
    Western Jin (265–317)
    Eastern Jin (317–420)
Southern and Northern Dynasties (Period of Disunity)
    South: Liu Sung (420–479)
        Qi (479–502)
        Liang (502–557)
        Zhen (557–589)
    North: Later (Northern) Wei (386–535)

Eastern Wei (534–550)
Western Wei (535–556)
Northern Qi (550–577)
Northern Zhou (557–581)
Sui Dynasty (590–618)
Tang Dynasty (618–906)
Five Dynasties (907–960)
    Later Liang (907–923)
    Later Tang (923–936)
    Later Jin (936–947)
    Later Han (947–950)
    Later Zhou (951–960)
Song Dynasty (960–1279)
    Northern Song (960–1126)
    Southern Song (1127–1279)
    Liao (907–1125)
    Western Xia (990–1227)
    Zin (1115–1234)
Yuan Dynasty (Mongols) (1260–1368)
Ming Dynasty (1368–1644)
Qing Dynasty (Manchus) (1644–1912)
Republic (1912–1949)
    Guomingdang (1928–1949)
        in Taiwan (1949–)
People's Republic (1949–)

1

TO
OPEN
THE
SUBJECT:
THE
DA GUAN YUAN

What garden could be more captivating than the Da Guan Yuan (Grand View Garden) described in the book *A Dream of the Red Chamber*? In it were hills, ponds, and brooks, exotic flowers and shrubs, as well as an assortment of storks, deer, rabbits, ducks, and geese to embellish the scenery. It contained a thousand and one scenes, each with a different emotional appeal. The Yi Hong Yuan (Happy Red Court), for one, in which Jia Baoyu lived, was a labyrinthian maze of buildings appointed with luxurious and classic elegance and set off by flowering shrubs and trees that gave off a multiplicity of fragrances. It is described in the seventeenth chapter of the book in the following manner:

[Jia Zheng and others went] past some double-flowering peach in blossom and through a moon gate made of bamboo over which climbed flowering plants. Whitewashed walls and green willows confronted them then. Along the walls ran covered corridors, and the rockery in the center of the courtyard was flanked on one side by plantains, on the other by a red multipetalled crab apple tree, its branches trained in the shape of an umbrella, with green trailing tendrils and petals red as cinnabar. . . . [Jia Zheng] led the way into the building. It was unusually set out with no clear-cut divisions between the different rooms. There were only partitions formed of shelves for books, bronze tripods, stationery, flower vases, and miniature gardens, some round, some square, some shaped like sunflowers, plantain leaves, or intersecting arcs.

They were beautifully carved with the motifs "clouds and a hundred bats" or the "three companions of winter"—pine, plum, and bamboo—as well as landscapes and figures, birds and flowers, scroll-work, imitation curios, and symbols of good fortune or long life. All executed by the finest craftsmen, they were brilliantly colored and inlaid with gold or precious stones. The effect was splendid, the workmanship exquisite. Here a strip of colored gauze concealed a small window, there a gorgeous curtain hid a door. There were also niches on the walls to fit antiques, lyres, swords, vases, or other ornaments, which hung level with the surface of the wall. . . . After passing two partitions Jia Zheng and his party lost their way. To their left they saw a door, to their right a window; but when they went forward their passage was blocked by a bookshelf. Turning back they glimpsed the way through another window; but on reaching the door they suddenly saw a party just like their own confronting them—they were looking at a big mirror. Passing round this they came to more doorways. . . .

Woodcut illustration from the novel "A Story of the Stone" in the Chinese classic, *A Dream of the Red Chamber.*

Entirely different from the Yi Hong Yuan in taste and interest was the Dao Xiang Cun (Paddy-Sweet Cottage) where Li Wan lived. Rustic and idyllic in tone, it was described in the book as follows:

. . . their eyes fell on some green hills barring their way. Skirting these they caught sight of brown adobe walls with paddy-stalk copings and hundreds of apricot trees, their blossoms bright as spurting flames or sunlit clouds. Inside this enclosure stood several thatched cottages. Outside grew saplings of mulberry, elm, hibiscus, and silkworm-thorn trees, whose branches had been intertwined to form a double green hedge. Beyond this hedge, at the foot of the slope, was a rustic well complete with windlass and well sweep. Below, neat plots of fine vegetables and rape flowers stretched as far as the eye could see.

On the top of a flowering apricot tree here hung a tavern sign; chickens and geese ran about in the yards and surrounding fields—one saw a tableau straight out of the pastoral poetry of Fan Shihu. Interest-provoking too, each in its own way, were other landscapes in the Da Guan Yuan: the Xiao Xiang Guan, encircled by a clear-flowing stream and green bamboos, and the Heng Wu Yuan, nestling in the midst of hills redolent of the perfume of a hundred flowers. Classical Chinese gardens—the larger ones—always contained many smaller ones, all different in tone and point of interest. This characteristic gained them the reputation of being "gardens within gardens."

Despite the profusion of landscapes it embodied, the Da Guan Yuan did not take up much space. It measured no more than three and a half *li* (2.79 square yards or 2.33 square meters) in circumference. Chinese classical gardens were very often laid out on extremely small plots of land. But the visitor who walks through their intricate recesses feels himself transported in the midst of an infinite variety of scenes. This can be attributed to one of the specialties of Chinese landscape gardening—the ability, as in certain types of Chinese painting, to create a given effect or feeling with a minimum of means.

Not only such private gardens as the Da Guan Yuan, but most Chinese classical gardens are indisputably beautiful. The palace gardens of China's successive kings and emperors are particularly impressive. Enclosing large tracts of land within their walls, they could be designed to achieve a sense of greater freedom and space and to create entirely different effects. Then there are the famous scenic areas whose natural possibilities were exploited and developed down through the years by Buddhist monasteries and Taoist temples. These scenic gardens, which were adapted to the existing contours and beauties of the environment, are a Chinese garden type with a particularly natural flavor to them. Aside from these, scenic spots in cities or their nearby suburbs have been built into excursion centers with a natural setting since ancient times. Examples of these are Qu Jiang in the city of Changan (today Xi'an), constructed during the Tang period; the Jin Ming Chi in the city of Bianliang (today Kaifeng), dating from the Northern Song dynasty; Xi Hu (West Lake) in the city of Linan (today Hangzhou), built during the Southern Song dynasty; Shi Sha Hai in Beijing, dating from the Ming and Qing dynasties; and Daming Lake in the city of Jinan. Although some of these places contained villas, resorts, and other buildings meant for the use of emperors, kings, and the rich and powerful, they were nevertheless used as public gardens to which city people flocked on holidays and in fine weather.

Since China is a vast country with marked geographical and cultural differences between her northern and southern regions, the styles of landscape gardening vary considerably. Gardens in the north, for instance, tend toward staidness, dignity, and grandeur; those south of the Changjiang (Yangtze) River are more delicate, refined, elegant, and flexible; while in southern China they are characterized by ebullience and piquancy.

China's civilization flourished relatively early. On her broad and richly endowed lands, an industrious people labored generation after generation to develop her resources and create material wealth. Their creativeness also extended to culture and art, and several thousand years of endeavor in this field has borne fruit, producing a rich national culture. Broad and profound in content, unique in style and form, this culture has contributed much to the treasures of human civilization. A shining jewel in China's cultural heritage is the art of landscape gardening. Garden construction and management are not Chinese alone, but if the level of understanding of, and degree of mastery in, the art are taken into account, China's landscape gardening possesses certain unique and original aspects not found in other cultures.

2
A
STROLL
IN
A
PICTURE:
THE
YI HE YUAN
OF
THE
SUMMER
PALACE

When Granny Liu entered the Da Guan Yuan, she was bewildered and awestricken by the intricate and constantly changing scenes that met her eyes. And in reply to the lady dowager's question as to what she thought of the garden, she exclaimed: "Gracious Buddha! We country folk come to town before New Year to buy pictures to stick up, and when we're at loose ends we often say, 'If only we could take a stroll in these pictures!' We always reckoned the places shown were too good to be true, but coming to this garden today I can see it is ten times better than any painting." Granny Liu's words were simple but to the point, for that is just what a Chinese garden is like. To be regarded as a masterpiece, it must be as carefully composed and executed as a picture. And what is more, it must possess certain poetic qualities. Thus Chinese gardens may be described as "embodied poems and three-dimensional pictures."

Before we discuss them any further, let us go for a visit to one of these three-dimensional picture-poems, to that splendid and tranquilly beautiful palace resort, the Yi He Yuan.

After setting out from the ancient yet youthful city of Beijing and driving northwest approximately six miles (ten kilometers), we reach the well-known Yi He Yuan, the Summer Palace. It was built in the early years of the Qing dynasty (1644–1912) by the Emperor Qian Long to celebrate his mother's birthday. Then called the Qing You Yuan (Qing Park), it was renamed Yi He Yuan in the final years of the dynasty, when the Empress Dowager Ci Xi (Tz'u Hsi), a lover of pleasure gardens, appropriated funds destined for the navy to rebuild it in honor of her sixtieth birthday. The Yi He Yuan today appears as it was rebuilt during that period.

As we approach our destination, and before

we see the Summer Palace's main gate, we are
greeted by the sight of a gorgeously painted three-
bay wooden archway straddling the road. This sig-
nals our arrival at Yi He Yuan. Through it and
a turn later, we come to the square before the Dong
Gong Men (East Palace Gate).

Dong Gong Men is the Summer Palace's main
gate. A five-bay construction, it rests on a white
marble foundation. Steps and an "imperial pathway" consisting of a single big slab of stone carved
with a dragon-and-clouds design lead up to the
three-bay doorway. In front of the gate stands a
brace of finely wrought bronze lions, and on either
side are two wicket gates. In front of the gate is
a large ochre red screen wall. To the left and right
are rows of buildings, one on each side, that once
served the guards at the gate as duty offices. These,
the screen wall, and the gate enclose the square.

Today we can saunter nonchalantly through
the main gate, since Yi He Yuan is now a public
park. It was, of course, forbidden to the common
people during the Qing dynasty, and even palace
attendants and ministers summoned to audiences
had to use the side gates. The main gate was reserved for the empress dowager, the emperor, and
his consorts.

Inside the main gate is a yard planted with
stately pines and cypresses, and straight ahead is
a second gate over which hangs a placard inscribed
with the words *Ren Shou Men* (Gate of Benevolence
and Longevity). Just inside this gate is a large
ornamental rock, and on either side of the yard we
see bronze dragons, phoenixes, jars, and *ding,* a

Bronze dragon and phoenix in front of the Hall
of Benevolence and Longevity.

kind of ancient cooking vessel, as well as flowers
and rockeries. The central building in the yard is
the Ren Shou Dian (Hall of Benevolence and Longevity), a magnificent structure in which matters
of state were administered. It still retains an air
of regal solemnity in spite of the flowers and ornaments that embellish it. From this precisely arranged yard, two paths lead farther into the park.
The path south of the hall seems to be a lesser
pathway, since it is obstructed by a hill. But as
we follow its meanderings, the view suddenly
broadens to reveal the waters of Kunming Lake,
blue as the sky above them, delicately setting off
the sumptuous coloration of Wan Shou Shan, the
Hill of Longevity. The distant Western Hills and
the slim pagoda on Yu Quan Shan (Jade Fountain
Hill), all lightly veiled in mist, provide a dignified
yet lavish backdrop for the whole scene.

Hall of Benevolence and Longevity.

The other path leads north from the Hall of Benevolence and Longevity, past a courtyard with tall buildings—De He Yuan, or Garden of Virtuous Harmony. The main structure inside this yard is Yi Le Dian, or Hall of Pleasant Entertainment, and facing it stands a magnificent multistoried stage. On its three tiers, simultaneous performances were once given. Superbly designed, it contained a variety of props and contrivances for special effects. Farther to the northeast, the path continues up the Hill of Longevity.

Behind and against the Hall of Benevolence and Longevity lies Yu Lan Tang, the Hall of Jade Ripples, a quiet, elegant courtyard designed for human habitation. It was used by Ci Xi as a special prison for the Emperor Guang Xu after the suppression of the Reform Movement of 1898, and to this day visitors can see the grim wall of gray brick that seals the windows of its western wing. Behind this hall stand several groups of residential buildings— Yi Yun Guan (Studio of Delightful Arts), Ou Xiang Xie (Pavilion of the Fragrance of Lotus), and Xi Jia Lou (House of Evening Splendor), all admirably adapted to the surrounding scenery. As the name implies, the House of Evening Splendor was a place from which to admire the setting sun back-lighting the somberly majestic Western Hills.

West of the Garden of Virtuous Harmony stands Le Shou Tang (Hall of Happy Longevity). This used to be the living quarters of Ci Xi and counterpart of her official residence in the Forbidden City, whereas Ren Shou Dian, inside the main gate, served as the audience hall of this imperial summer resort. This arrangement, in fact, retained the principle of the imperial palaces—"audience halls in front and living quarters behind"—but applied it with more flexibility. Le Shou Tang consists of two precisely laid out courtyards, the main buildings and wings of which are connected with covered walks, allowing the inhabitants to pass from one building to another sheltered from sun and rain. This device was commonly employed in classical Chinese architecture. Chinese crab apple trees, magnolias, and other flowering trees are planted in the courtyards and each spring burst out in magnificent many-hued banks of blossoms. Also here are ancient bronze sculptures of deer and stork—symbols of longevity—as well as rocks, flowers, and miniature potted gardens. The famous rock, Qing Zhi Xiu (Black Ornamental Mountain),

The famous rock, Qing Zhi Xiu (Black Ornamental Mountain) in the courtyard of Le Shou Tang (Hall of Happy Longevity).

Windows of many shapes looking out toward the
lake in the outer courtyard of Le Shou Tang.

The Fan-shaped Hall seen through the moon gate.

stands in the front courtyard. The decorative work on the buildings as well as the furnishings and exhibits inside, luxurious and extremely valuable, were produced by the skilled hands of famous artisans of the late Qing dynasty.

In front of Le Shou Tang is the imperial wharf. Here, beside the lake, once stood a brass lantern rack. Soaring high in the shape of a graceful arch, it served as a beacon for nighttime boaters. The pale pink walls of the covered walk fronting the outer courtyard of Le Shou Tang are perforated by a series of windows in the shapes of squares, crosses, diamonds, pentagons, fans, scrolls, plantain leaves, peaches, crab apples, pomegranates, and so forth. Lights were placed in them during nocturnal boating parties. These and their reflections on the lake waters, coupled with the lanterns on the dragon and phoenix boats rocking on the lake, created a veritable fairyland of lights. And on nights when fireworks were set off, the glistening waves on the lake, the red palace lanterns outlining the halls ensconced among dark pines, and the brilliantly lit boats set against a night sky tinted by the fireworks created a spectacle that surpasses all description.

Proceeding from Le Shou Tang, we come upon an enchanting little courtyard. Peering through the moon gate, we can see on the other side of a pond a pine-overgrown hill with a small building on it. Named Yang Ren Feng (Breeze of Benevolence), the building was ingeniously designed in the shape of a fan to evoke the words "raising the breeze of benevolence," a quotation from the *Book of Jin: Biography of Yuan Hong,* meaning that the Confucianist spirit of benevolence and love should be

The Fan-shaped Hall, also called Yang Ren Feng (Raising the Breeze of Benevolence).

Chang Lang, the Long Corridor.

25

observed in ruling the populace. The building is generally known as the Fan-shaped Hall.

Farther to the west, we reach the famous Chang Lang (Long Corridor). A structure with more than two hundred bays, it meanders for 766 yards (700 meters) along the southern foot of the Hill of Longevity, and its magnificence brings to mind descriptions of the fabled A Fang Palace of the ancient Qin dynasty. It is one of the chief tourist attractions, with its breathtaking lake scenes seen through "picture frames" formed by the pillars, railings, and crossbeams of the corridor. Closer at hand, as we walk along the corridor, we can enjoy the pictures painted on the beams and crosspieces of the walk. Known as Suzhou-style paintings, they cover a wide range of subject matter: everything from flowers, birds and beasts, and landscapes to legends, opera scenes, and historic events. Those who are interested tarry a while and try to identify the stories represented in the pictures—stories such as "Three Visits to the Cottage," "Meeting on the Terrace," and "Daiyu Buries Flowers." When several people do this, it resembles the Chinese party game in which players guess riddles pasted over lanterns.

One may feel tired after walking such a long distance. The designers of the corridor, those master craftsmen of days gone by, have provided for such a contingency. As they built this covered walkway to enable us to admire the scenery sheltered from sunshine, rain, or snow, they also lined its entire length with a benchlike balustrade so that we might sit down whenever we feel like taking a rest.

Walking to the western end of the Long Corridor, we are greeted by the sight of a large pleasure boat in the lake. It cannot sail away, however, since it is actually a boat-shaped building constructed in the water. Named Qing Yan Fang (Qing Banquet Boat), it is better known simply as Shi Fang, or Marble Boat. Dating from the reign of Emperor Qian Long, it can now be seen as it was rebuilt in the last years of the Qing dynasty. Architecturally it is rather peculiar, with its many Western characteristics. Boat-shaped buildings are an interesting innovation frequently seen in Chinese gardens, particularly in the private gardens south of the Changjiang (Yangtze) River, where the small size of the lakes precludes the pleasures of boating and such "land ships" were built beside the water to simulate the experience. At Yu Yuan (Garden of Pleasure) in Shanghai, one of these boats was built entirely on dry land. Although no water surrounds it, the boatlike appurtenances seem to create a quiet lake scene by mental association, and the occupants sense something of the carefree enjoyment of sailing on a lake. This may be likened to Chinese traditional opera, in which the actors make use of a symbolic oar and dance movements to give the audience an impression that the action takes place on a lake or river. Chinese artists are well versed in creating certain effects with minimal means.

The frontal slope of the Hill of Longevity is the hub of the park and embodies the cream of its architecture. Here, the sculptured marble balustrade and the Long Corridor along the lakeside serve to set off the green hill and its pavilions and ter-

The Marble Boat.

A pleasure boat on the Kunming Lake.

races. Seen from the lake, it seems to be resting upon an elegant platter and so takes on greater distinction. The layout of the front slope revolves around a central axis, which extends from the Yun Hui Yu Yu (Brilliant Clouds and Jade Universe) ceremonial arch by the lakeside through Pai Yun Men (Cloud-Dispelling Gate) and Pai Yun Dian (Cloud-Dispelling Hall) up to the imposing Fo Xiang Ge (Temple of Buddhist Virtue) near the top of the hill. This last, an octagonal four-story structure, is the focus of the park's layout and dominates the scene. It establishes a sense of unified order and precedence among the multifarious pavilions, terraces, and buildings. With its encircling gallery, shining, yellow-glazed tiles, and golden

crown hung with tinkling bells, all set off by the well-balanced and majestic base upon which it stands, Fo Xiang Ge has the appearance of those multistoried buildings often seen in Song dynasty paintings. Those who go inside will find a hall for the worship of Sakyamuni, put there by the reigning feudal dynasty to evoke good fortune.

Standing on the southern side of the lofty base of Fo Xiang Ge, we see in the distance the Kunming Lake with the Long Wang Miao (Dragon King's Temple) on an island in its center, six bridges on a dyke along the western side of the lake, and pleasure boats drifting here and there. The scene is very much like that at the West Lake in Hangzhou. It used to be said that "above us there is Paradise; and here below we have Suzhou and Hangzhou." In former days the beauty and elegance of the seven-*li* (5.48 square yards or 4.66 square meters) Shan Tang from the city of Suzhou to Hu Qiu (Tiger Hill) and the West Lake under the walls of Hangzhou attracted flocks of visitors. After the Emperor Qian Long made a tour south of the Changjiang River, he was so enamored of what he had seen in Hangzhou and Suzhou that he ordered facsimiles constructed at this Qing dynasty palace. The front lake was built to resemble the West Lake, and the back lake to look like the Shan Tang. To the west of the front, or Kunming, lake, clouds blazing in the rays of the setting sun accentuate the ever shifting purples, blues, and brownish grays of undulating Western Hills that seem to form a unity with the scenery in the park. To the southwest we can see verdant fields and the city of Beijing

Pai Yun Dian (Cloud-Dispelling Hall) and the
Kunming Lake, as seen from Fo Xiang Ge (Temple
of Buddhist Virtue).

and its outskirts. And on clear days we are regaled with the sight of ancient gate-towers, white pagodas, the Coal Hill, and the palaces of the Forbidden City, as well as tall buildings of more recent construction, all nestling among the trees of Beijing. Lowering our eyes from this delightful view, we see the buildings of the Pai Yun Dian complex marching down the southern foot of the Hill of Longevity in orderly rows along the axial line of Fo Xiang Ge. The yellow tiles, red walls, green trees, and white balustrades blend like a brocade fabric that stretches right down to the lakeside.

Fo Xiang Ge is set off by a number of other buildings. Behind it, on the summit of the hill, stands Zhi Hui Hai (Wisdom Sea Temple), a five-bay hall fronted by a three-bay ceremonial arch with a facing of glazed tiles. The hall itself is also entirely decorated with polychromatic glazed tiles. The outer walls are inlaid with countless little glazed Buddhas that glitter splendidly in the sunlight. On the left of Fo Xiang Ge is a building named Zhuan Lun Zang (Repository of Buddhist Sutras). On the right stands Wu Fang Ge (Pentagonal Pavilion) and the Bronze House. Below these lies a large rockery, the stones of which follow the contours of the slope and form a labyrinthian maze of tunnels, caves, and convoluted paths.

The front of the Hill of Longevity, both east and west of Fo Xiang Ge, is adorned with a score of buildings or clusters of buildings each with its own point of interest. On the eastern side, for instance, we have Yang Yun Xuan (Cloud Nurturing Arbor), Chun Yi Xuan (Anticipate the Spring Arbor), Xie Qiu Xuan (Arbor for Depicting Autumn Scenes), Yuan Lang Zhai (House of Spacious Gardens), Yi Chi Yun Zai (Clouds Beautiful Beyond Comparison), Jing Fu Ge (Abode of Beautiful Scenes), and others; while to the west we find Yun Song Chao (Abode of Clouds and Pines), Shao Wo (Eminent Hideout), Ting Li Guan (Listen-to-the-Orioles Studio), Hua Zhong You (Strolling in Scenery), Hu Shan Zhen Yi (True Picture of the Lake and Mountains), Gui Shou Wu Ji (Unlimited Longevity), Ji Lan Tang (Hall on the Billows), Ying Xu Lou (Greet-the-Rising-Sun Tower), Cheng Huai Ge (Abode of the Clear Mind), and more. All are exquisitely constructed and surrounded with flowers and trees. So profuse and varied are the scenes they represent that one must go there personally to visualize them.

After entering the main gate of the Summer Palace, a short walk along the eastern bank of the lake brings us to a small island linked to the shore by a flat wooden bridge with vermilion balustrades. On the island stands an open, square-shaped pavilion with multiple eaves. It is called Zhi Chun Ting (Spring-Heralding Pavilion), after the lines "the ducks are first to herald the warming of the waters in spring" in the poem written by Su Dongpo (A.D. 1036–1101) of the Song dynasty. Weeping willows planted among the rocks scattered around the pavilion sway gracefully in the breeze. In these leisurely surroundings, the visitor may enjoy scenes of the Summer Palace, enframed by the pillars and crossbeams of the pavilion: to the north we see the Hill of Longevity, and to the

Zhi Hui Hai (Wisdom Sea Temple), with its facing
of glazed tiles, at the top of the Hill of Longevity.

The Jade Fountain Hill and the Western Hills, as seen from Hu Shan Zhen Yi (True Picture of the Lake and Mountains).

south is the large island with the Dragon King's Temple as well as the Seventeen-Arch Bridge.

Walking farther south along the lake bank we pass through a small gate surmounted with a dainty yet dignified gate tower: Wen Chang Ge (Pavilion of Flourishing Culture). The bank here is lined with weeping willows, the low-hanging branches of which caress the surface of the water. Through this latticework of hanging green branches, we see the Western Hills, misty blue in the distance, marked off from the lake waters by a long, green dyke punctuated here and there with bridges. The scene here most resembles that at the West Lake at Hangzhou. A swimming area has now been demarcated here, next to the Wen Chang Ge, and visitors are afforded the pleasure of bathing in the rippling waters of Kunming Lake.

Farther south, just before coming to the Seventeen-Arch Bridge, we find a bronze ox—Zhen Hai Niu (Calm-the-Seas Ox)—staidly reclining on a carved Sumeru pedestal of white marble. The ox, vividly executed, seems to be contemplating the broad expanse of Kunming Lake. Listed as a cultural relic, it is one of the better works of bronze sculpture of the Qing dynasty period.

A few steps farther bring us to the white marble Seventeen-Arch Bridge. At the head of the bridge stands a lofty pavilion named Lang Ru Ting (Veranda-like Pavilion), sometimes called Ba Fang Ting (Eight-Direction Pavilion), which, together with the bridge and the island, forms a balanced pictorial composition. At the other end of the bridge lies the largest island on the lake, sur-mounted by Long Wang Miao (Dragon King's Temple), Han Xu Tang (Hall of Modesty), Yue Po Lou (House of Moonlit Waves), Jian Yuan Tang (Hall of the Enjoyment of Distant Scenes), and other buildings. From the lake, the island, with its superimposed buildings rising mist-enshrouded from the waves, resembles the magic island in the sea described in fairy tales and legends.

The surface of the Kunming Lake covers an area of about 5.7 acres (2.5 hectares) and occupies three-quarters of the park. Its fresh and pure serenity, contrasted with the opulence of the Hill of Longevity, gives the park the charm of a masterpiece of scenic painting. Aside from the island just mentioned and another one called Feng Huang Dun (Phoenix Mound) in the southern part of the lake, a long dyke stretches north to south across the western side of Kunming Lake. Built in imitation of the Su Dyke at the West Lake in Hangzhou, it has six bridges on it—Xiu Yi Qiao (Bridge of Exquisite Ripples), Liu Qiao (Willow Bridge), Lian Qiao (White Silk Bridge), Jing Qiao (Mirror Bridge), Yu Dai Qiao (Jade Belt Bridge), and Bin Feng Qiao (*Bin* Style Bridge). These bridges, either flat and surmounted by painted pavilions or built of white marble in the shape of a single arched span, present a picturesque sight standing as they do over the water against a backdrop of mountains. The dyke itself is planted over with weeping willows interspersed with peach trees, and when the peach trees blossom in spring, the pink flowers against the green of the willows re-create the beauty of the countryside south of the Changjiang River. Aquatic

Wen Chang Ge (Pavilion of Flourishing Culture).

Yu Dai Qiao (Jade Belt Bridge), crossing the western part of Kunming Lake.

Zhi Chun Ting (Spring-Heralding Pavilion).

The bronze ox and the Seventeen-Arch Bridge.

A painted pavilion-bridge.

Another pavilion on a bridge of the western dyke of Kunming Lake.

plants such as water chestnut, lotus, cattail, and bullrush grow in the water next to the dyke and add a natural touch to the scenery. On the western side of the dyke lies another lake, itself divided into two sections by a shorter dyke. Each section has an islet in it, with buildings and terraces constructed in imitation of the "fairy mountains in the sea" seen in gardens of the Han and Tang dynasties.

We can walk northward along the west dyke all the way to the back of the Hill of Longevity. A branch of the lake, extending to this place, is known as Hou Hu, or Back Lake. Long and narrow, the lake surface widens in places to form a chain of small lakes, giving the sailor the impression of passing through a series of courtyards. The banks of the central section of Back Lake were once lined with precise replicas of the singsong houses, taverns, teahouses, secondhand clothing stores, and curio shops along Suzhou's Shan Tang Street. So true to life were they that this section of Back Lake came to be known as the Suzhou River or Suzhou Street. The garden builders of the Qing dynasty showed remarkable inventiveness here; unfortunately, their creations were burned down by invading foreign troops in the last hundred years.

Also here, a single-span stone arch bridge leads straight to the north gate of the palace. Behind the bridge is a path up the back of the Hill of Longevity, near the summit of which stands Xu Mi Ling Jing (Sumeru Sanctuary), a group of buildings constructed in the stately Tibetan style. The entire landscaping at the back of the hill is designed to create an atmosphere of deep and quiet seclusion,

The Back Lake of the Summer Palace, Hou Hu.

A section of the Back Lake known as the Suzhou River.

Sumeru Sanctuary, a lamasery behind the Hill of Longevity.

with ancient temples in remote nooks, narrow winding paths, slopes ending abruptly beside clear, still waters, and towering trees on the wooded banks from which issue the calls of birds. The sharp contrast between the quiet, natural serenity of Back Lake and the magnificence of the front of the hill contributes to the diversity and enchantment of the park's scenery.

As we emerge from the small valleys with their feathered inhabitants, fragrance of lotus, and tiny streams, the view broadens out at the top of the hill. Clear blue skies and a fresh breeze blowing through the green trees have a marvelously bracing effect. Looking northward, we see farmland stretching to a range of precipitous blue mountains in the distance. The peach blossoms behind the Hill of Longevity are matchless: when they come in full bloom in early April, they bedeck the slopes and valleys with their splendor and bring to the park a joyous touch of spring.

Moving onward to the eastern foot of the hill, we come to Xie Qu Yuan, the Garden of Harmonious Delights. This is an exquisite little "waterscape" garden built on the model of Ji Chang Garden at Huishan, Wuxi. This garden within a garden consists of halls, pavilions, and covered walks arranged around a lotus-filled pond with banks of natural rock. As we stroll down from the mountain paths and peer through the ornate gate of the garden, we see among the variously shaped buildings and under the large, flat lotus leaves a stretch of clear water. This, and the shade from the surrounding trees, make the garden an admi-rable summer retreat, for even on the hottest days, they create coolness in the pavilions and covered walks.

Next to the pond stands a grove of graceful bamboos, whose leaves rustle softly in the moist, lotus-scented breeze. Here, as if the inverted reflections of the bamboos were not enough to hold our interest, the natural music of the wind plays upon a myriad of closely spaced canes. Now, come closer and listen! From the depths of the bamboo grove and through the curtain of green foliage comes the tinkling of flowing water—a most harmonious accompaniment to the tunes from the bamboos. Curiosity may impel you to search for the musical waters. If so, following a rivulet will lead you to a secluded little gully with weather-beaten trees growing between its silent, rocky walls. A clear stream courses among the boulders, sometimes slower, sometimes faster; as it splashes down from different heights upon the rocks, it produces sounds of varying pitch and intensity—thus the musical effect. This scene will fill you with admiration for the handiwork of nature, until you remember that these marvels were the work of human hands.

Xie Qu Yuan was constructed in the heyday of the Qing dynasty. When Qing You Yuan, precursor of the Summer Palace, was being built, the Emperor Qian Long took a trip to the south and visited the famous ancient garden of Wuxi, the Ji Chang Garden. He became so deeply attached to it that he had Xie Qu Yuan built in the same manner. The scenic layout of Xie Qu Yuan is fundamentally the same as that of the older garden: it also has a sector for water scenery and another for hill scenery. But it was executed with certain variations, and the architecture is wholly palatial in tone. The Ji Chang Garden had in its hill sector a "gully of eight sounds." This was a winding little ravine constructed, in an exaggerated style, by piling rocks on a man-made earthen hill. Through it was led a stream of water, and along its course eight pools were placed at different heights so that the water produced different sounds as it fell into them. The purpose was to create an illusion of idyllic seclusion. The modified version in Xie Qu Yuan made partial use of the existing natural environment and was done in a style more realistic and true to nature, so that man's intervention is hardly noticeable. In approach it differs from the Ji Chang Garden, but the result is equally satisfactory.

Proceeding southward from Xie Qu Yuan, we soon return to the main gate of the Summer Palace. And after this brief visit, during which we have gained a rough idea of the park, we are ready to depart. But a first visit to the Summer Palace is apt to kindle a lasting nostalgia. As it is when one hears a beautiful piece of music, a visit to a lovely garden often leaves lingering echoes in one's soul. A large and finely built park like the Summer Palace is bound to contain many original and ingenious features, and although you may gain a general impression of them in the course of such a cursory examination, maximum aesthetic enjoyment can be obtained only from a more leisurely appreciation. You will be spiritually the richer if you peruse the classical Chinese garden as you do a poem or a picture.

Winding path on a crag.

Yu Qin Xia rocks.

CREATING "EMBODIED POEMS AND THREE-DIMENSIONAL PICTURES": THE PRINCIPLES OF CHINESE GARDEN DESIGN

Those who have visited classical Chinese gardens were perhaps most impressed by the picturesque pavilions, terraces, covered walks, and many-storied buildings scattered over the landscape, half-hidden by trees and flowering shrubs; or by the winding paths leading to quiet retreats by the lakes rippling amidst green hills, the broad expanses of lotus flowers swaying in the wind, and the springs bubbling in wooded dells. And indeed, these are the sort of things in which Chinese landscape gardening excels. Chinese garden builders pay particular attention to composition. Not only must the garden as a whole revolve around a central theme, but every view and scene should also have its own point of interest and appeal, as does a painting or a piece of poetry. It has been said, and rightly so, that classical Chinese gardens are picturesque and poetic, for in their artistic qualities, they are pictures and poems expressed in the vocabulary of gardening. In other words these artificially created environments, which afford the visitor the delights of natural landscapes, may be likened to embodied poems that are both visible and tangible or to three-dimensional scenic paintings the viewer can walk right into.

If we wish to gain a deeper understanding and appreciation of Chinese gardens, we should first know how they are created. We shall briefly examine the principles that underlie their construction. First, let us consider some of the main elements that go into their makeup.

BUILDINGS: SIMPLE AND RICH GARDENHOUSES

In gardens, buildings are the chief means of affording the occupants shelter from sun and rain, as well as a place to rest. Since these buildings are likely to be the focus of attention, they are more often than not made the dominant feature of the pictorial composition.

The various types of buildings in Chinese classical gardens are closely integrated with the landscape and vegetation and treated as inseparable components of the garden as a whole. They were especially numerous in classical gardens, palatial and private, because of the actual daily needs of those who aspired to a rusticated life. In the gardens attached to imperial summer resorts, for instance,

Covered bridge makes right-angle turns through part of Bei Hai Park, Beijing.

Right:
A placard atop the main gate of the Summer Palace.

Left:
The main gate of the Summer Palace, Yi He Yuan.

Above:
Kunming Lake and the Hill of Longevity.

Right:
The multistoried stage in the courtyard of De He Yuan (Garden of Virtuous Harmony).

Left:
A picture on a beam in the
Long Corridor, Chang Lang.

Right:
The Bronze House atop the
Hill of Longevity.

Right:
Lang Ru Ting (Veranda-like Pavilion) and the Seventeen-Arch Bridge.

Left:

A panoramic view of Kunming Lake and the island on which stands the Dragon King's Temple.

Below left:

A pavilion in Liu Yuan (Garden to Linger In) of Suzhou.

Below right:

Xie Qu Yuan (Garden of Harmonious Delights) in spring.

Below:
A richly decorated pavilion in the Imperial Garden, Beijing, with carved balustrades, gilt-embellished beams and brackets under the eaves, vermilion pillars, and yellow glazed tiles.

Right:
A unicorn sculpture in the Imperial Garden, Beijing.

Opposite, above left:
A garden scene viewed through a window.

Opposite, above right:
A hole-window that serves as a picture frame.

Opposite, bottom:
The balustrades of this building serve to frame the scenery visible beyond.

Interior of the Hall for An-
tique Forests and Springs in
Suzhou's Liu Yuan.

were built groups of buildings for audience-giving and government administration similar to the great halls in the Imperial Palace in the capital, as well as residential buildings comparable to the official imperial bedchambers—all in addition to those constructions serving the needs of sightseers or required in scenic compositions. Private gardens, on the other hand, were mostly adjoined to the owners' residences—behind or to one side—and thus constituted what the layman would call backyards. Serving their owners as places for everyday activities, for pleasure, or for parties on festivals and special occasions, they too contained quite a number of pavilions, halls, and other such buildings.

Since buildings, unlike plants, are man-made and may be built in any desired shape and painted in various colors, they are one of the most handy and versatile elements of garden construction. Their number, size, style, and color have an important bearing on the tone and style of the garden, and the treatment they are given depends to a large extent on whether the garden is sylvan or rustic or resplendent with gorgeous vegetation and magnificent architecture.

In the private gardens of south China, for instance, deep-hued tiled roofs and cheerful whitewashed walls are set off by green plantains and bamboos amid light gray rocks and ponds mirroring the colors of the sky. And in all types of structures, be they covered walks, pavilions, halls, or multistoried buildings, the long, slender pillars and the imprecisely proportioned—yet for that all the more unpretentious and appealing—beams and cross-pieces are painted jet black. This gives the buildings the appearance of having been traced and outlined in black ink and, against the green trees and blue sky, reproduces the tone of restrained elegance seen in Chinese ink-and-wash paintings.

An entirely different style is found at the Summer Palace in Beijing. At strategic spots among the blue waves of the Kunming Lake and the luxuriant green foliage of the Hill of Longevity are disposed groups of richly decorated buildings reminiscent of the gold-and-green landscape paintings of the Song dynasty. Ordinary buildings in the Summer Palace are done in natural shades of gray and green to blend into the quiet lake-and-mountain landscapes. But in order to create a sense of grandeur consistent with an imperial garden, key buildings in the palace section and in the scenic composition are given special treatment as regards form and coloring. Here one finds the roofs of dazzling yellow-glazed tiles set off by green foliage and blue skies; the gilt-embellished multicolored beams and brackets under the eaves; the rows of vermilion pillars; the white, carved balustrades and marble inlays; the many black tablets with gold lettering and borders; the bronze dragons, phoenixes, jars, sacrificial vessels, and other such sculptures arrayed before the buildings. It goes without saying that such things were reserved for the type of garden built for the emperors and kings of old.

Apart from such differences that exist between the buildings of private and palace gardens and of north and south China, the form and tone of architecture also vary with the *leitmotiv* of the land-

Detail of the Five Dragons Pavilions in Bei Hai
Park, Beijing.

A many-storied building in Suzhou's Liu Yuan.

Ke Ting, a pavilion in Suzhou's Liu Yuan.

A wall climbing the hill, Hangzhou's Xi Leng (Seal-Engravers' Club).

scapes. In gardens with a pastoral theme, for instance, the buildings are done in a rustic wood-and-thatch style. In classical gardens the architecture itself has characteristics that suit the natural setting. Some types were designed to fit in with mountain scenes, others with bodies of water, resulting in many types of buildings: *ting* (pavilions), *lang* (covered walks or corridors), *xuan* (verandas with windows), *xie* (waterside pavilions), *ting tang* (halls), *lou ge* (multistoried buildings), *han chuan* (land boats), *yun qiang* (walls with cloud designs), *qu qiao* (curved bridges), *ting qiao* (bridges sur-mounted by pavilions), *lang qiao* (covered bridges), and so on. Their dimensions and proportions were adapted to those of the natural surroundings. Buildings in gardens also had to be better than average in decor and spatial arrangement.

PLANTS: A MOST USEFUL NATURAL RESOURCE

The treatment of vegetation, under the overall thinking that guided the construction of classical

A covered walk in Bei Hai Park in Beijing.

Swallows-Arriving Pavilion, Tian Ping Mountain, Suzhou.

Chinese garden construction, this consists chiefly of making judicious use of their shape, color, odor, and acoustic properties (activated by wind and rain) to enhance the artistic effect of a desired scenic environment.

Take, for instance, the acoustic properties of plants. A garden can be given a highly poetic atmosphere by placing in it certain large-leaved plants for the sound they give off when wind or rain beats upon them. The pattering of raindrops on a grove of plantains or on a few Chinese parasol trees planted under a window creates a sense of the unbounded stillness of nature—a source of inspiration for the poetically minded. And what better medium can one find for listening to the sound of rain than a lotus pond? Reluctant to have the withered lotus leaves in a pond cleared away in autumn, a poet once wrote, "Keep the remaining lotus leaves, that I may listen to the sound of rain." Pines and bamboo, on the other hand, are planted for the sound of the wind in their branches. It has been said, "The pipes of heaven sing when wind blows through the pines." The soughing of wind in a pine grove gives a garden landscape the appeal of a remote valley in the mountains. And nothing is so restful as the sound produced by swaying bamboos. Plants of the bamboo family are also a good medium for listening to the sound of rain.

With changes in the weather and time of day—wind or rain, clear days or cloudy, dawn or dusk—plants produce different effects as regards appearance, coloring, odor, and acoustics; and as the seasons go by they put forth leaves, flower, bear

Chinese gardens, differs from that of the West. The role of plants is not the same as that of buildings in the composition of a garden. Plants are one of the primary constituents of natural landscapes. They affect the microclimate by regulating temperature and humidity. Employed in the art of garden building, they are unquestionably the most effective element in the composition of garden landscapes.

Plants are a prerequisite in the formation of a garden environment. Generally speaking, however, the use of plant life in the restricted space of a garden is kept within limits, and their arrangement is subject to certain rules. In classical

Bananas are planted at the corner of a wall to catch the sound of the breeze, yet are sheltered from the full destructive force of the wind.

Bamboos.

fruit, or shed foliage. For this reason plants are used to bring out the seasonal characteristics of landscapes. In Chinese garden construction, therefore, the application of plant life embodies the important principle called "borrowing from the weather and the climate."

As in the creation of mountain and water landscapes, stress in the treatment of plants is laid not on quantity, but on whether or not, in the light of actual requirements, they suffice to convey the garden designer's intentions. Thus, in the relatively small gardens in city and town, their number is not as great as one might expect. Woods, for in-

stance, are represented by as few as four or five trees, strategically located according to the needs of the pictorial composition.

The species commonly used are those often depicted in poetry and paintings: bamboos, orchids, wintersweets, chrysanthemums, lotus, roses, peonies, plantains, Chinese parasol trees, plum trees, apricot trees, sweet-scented cassias, maples, and the like. These are selected and used according to such considerations as scenic theme, topography, and architectural surroundings. They serve both as a means of spatial control and as individual points of attraction.

Chinese wisteria planted in Suzhou's Wang Shi Yuan.

Loquat and tawny day lily.

HILLS: NOT THE HIGHER, THE BETTER

Pond digging is often accompanied by the use of earth and rocks to construct hills. From the construction engineer's standpoint, this is both rational and economical, for it balances the earthwork. In the landscaper's art, hills and bodies of water together often form the basic content of a garden landscape.

Hills are an effective means of achieving spatial control, particularly since they produce variations in elevation in the scenic sequence. In classical Chinese gardens, even minor rises in the terrain are generally characterized as hills; in the smaller gardens, the so-called hills are, from the viewpoint of earthwork, often mere mounds of earth. Hills need not be high; what counts is the sense of realism engendered by a combination of artistic effects: how their contours are designed, the arrangement of the paths winding among them, the placement of the rocks that rise above the vegetal cover, and the disposition of trees and shrubs whose shade produces a feeling of seclusion and depth. When used as a "mountains-in-the-distance" backdrop, hills of earth or rock serve simultaneously as the vanishing point of the garden's pictorial layout: they conceal the garden wall so that the viewer perceives only a stretch of green hills. The impression given is not that they mark the garden's limits, but that beyond their wooded undulations lie unlimited vistas. In this context artificial hills serve to create a feeling of greater space.

An enclosing wall on a hill of earth.

Forest on an artificial hill in Xie Qu Yuan, the Garden of Harmonious Delights.

Rockery and pathway in the Imperial Garden (Hou Yuan), Beijing.

In constructing artificial hills of rocks, as in house building, the stones may be laid in such a manner as to leave empty spaces (caves and tunnels) in the structure. Architecturally, and from the standpoint of artistic expression, this feature makes them most suitable for replicating the peaks, chasms, caves, precipices, and overhanging cliffs in nature. In practice, artificial rock hills are often pierced with tunnels and caves, sometimes with water flowing through them. Thus they can be viewed from within and without and afford greater variety than hills of earth.

A variation of the rock hill—the independent rocky promontory not connected with any range

A pile of rocks in garden construction.

A pond with stone balustrades, Xi Leng (Seal-Engravers' Club) in Hangzhou.

Another example of the use of piled rocks in garden building.

A rockery in the Imperial Garden (Hou Yuan).

of hills—is an ornamental object almost sculptural in quality. Called a *taihu* rock, this tall and exquisitely shaped solitary form still symbolizes a mountain peak in landscape gardening and is therefore laid out in line with the principles of mountain configuration. The Liu Garden in Suzhou is famous for its rocky "peaks"; all of its twelve original peaks consisted of carefully selected rocks from the region of the lake Tai Hu—whence the name *taihu* rock. The three peaks remaining there today—the Guan Yun (Crowning Clouds), Xiu Yun (Mountain in the Clouds), and Duo Yun (Clustered Clouds)—are still the largest of all the beautiful *taihu* rocks in the gardens of Suzhou. These strangely shaped decorative rocks were prized as garden embellishments as far back as the Tang dynasty (A.D. 618–906), and many valuable rocks were used in constructing the famous Gen Yu palace garden during the Northern Song dynasty (A.D. 960–1126). To enrich the scenery in this luxurious park, the imperial court sent out emissaries in search of famous flowers and exotic rocks, which were transported back to the capital, Daxing, in so-called flower-and-rock caravans. All along the way, houses were torn down, irrigation ditches leveled, and bridges built to facilitate transportation of the rocks, adding to the sufferings of the common people. This addiction to exotic rocks continued into the Qing dynasty period (1644–1912), when the four qualities *lou* (perforated), *tou* (transparent), *shou* (slender), and *zhou* (corrugated) were established as the aesthetic criteria for excellence.

Solitary rock peaks were often placed facing the doorway or window of a building, in the middle of a courtyard, or beside a bend in a path, where they served either as complementary embellishments to the view or as decorations in their own right. They also ornamented bodies of water, as in the case of the well-known Rock of the Beautiful Maiden, which stands in the middle of a pond at Wen Lan Ge Garden in Hangzhou. They were generally used in combination with flowers or as supports for climbing plants in imitation of the vine-festooned cliffs depicted in lyrical nature paintings.

WATER: MAKING THE SMALL EVOKE THE LARGE

Water is another important element in garden construction; in classical Chinese gardens in particular its use embodies some highly original modes of expression. As with hills, water has been given much importance by garden builders ever since the early days of the ancient art of garden construction in China. The general practice in creating hill-and-water landscapes was to exploit the natural environment as far as possible and improve upon it while retaining the natural flavor of the scenery.

Bodies of water in a garden have the salubrious functions of increasing atmospheric humidity and regulating the temperature. They can be used to raise fish, grow lotus, and provide such entertainment as fishing, boating, and, in winter, sledding and ice-skating. In combination with rocks and trees or pavilions, terraces, and other such buildings, they produce scenes of extraordinary liveliness and charm.

"Borrowing" the natural beauties of rivers, lakes, and the ocean is done wherever feasible in Chinese garden construction. In Wuxi, for instance, such gardens as the Li Yuan (Dipper Garden), Yu Zhuang (Fishing Village), and even the Mei Yuan (Plum Garden), which does not abut on the lake, are all constructed to bring the lovely scenery of

Tai Hu within their orbit—by the erection of pavilions and terraces from which the lake scenes may be seen and admired. In Beijing's Summer Palace, many of the buildings on the hill, such as the Hu Shan Zhen Yi (True Picture of Lake and Mountains), Jing Fu Ge (Abode of Beautiful Scenes), Xie Xiu Ting (Pavilion of Selected Elegance), and others are designed primarily to overlook the Kunming Lake. Needless to say, the same applies to the lakeside pavilions such as the Yu Zao Xuan (Fish and Algae Veranda), the Zhi Chun Ting (Spring-Heralding Pavilion), Xing Qiao (Bridge of Curves), and others. In these buildings the visitor is tempted to lean on the balustrades and, amidst the fragrance of lotus, admire the "shimmering waters of the placid lake, and the delectable charms of the mountains." Looking down, one sees graceful aquatic plants and, at night, the moon's reflection ready, as it were, to be scooped up from the still waters. One gets the feeling that the lake scenery, instead of surrounding the buildings, has been brought right into them. Here, water and architecture are so closely combined as to take the viewer into a world of poetry. Natural bodies of water, whether against a background of misty hills, a stretch of wooded land, or simply a clear blue sky, create an inimitable sense of restfulness and relaxation.

As with hills, in treating a body or bodies of water, one should not simply imitate natural phenomena, but should attempt to re-create nature in a lyrical and artistically succinct manner. The garden builder uses water to reproduce lakes, ponds, mountain streams, waterfalls, brooks, and springs.

A pond surrounded by rockery, Bei Hai Park, Beijing.

A ditch surrounded by rocks can create the illusion
of a mountainscape.

None of these, however, is created on a scale comparable to those in real life. All that is needed is the atmosphere. The seemingly boundless lake scene in the Wang Shi Yuan at Suzhou, for instance, actually covers an area of only one *mu* (809.7 square yards or 667 square meters). The Hao Pu Jian (Ravine Scene) in Beijing's Bei Hai Park seems to lead the visitor through a gorge deep in the mountains, though it is little more than a curved ditch with some water in it. In spite of their small size, these bodies of water create an impression of being actual scenes from nature, owing to their well-conceived configurations, the true-to-life arrangement of their banks, and the effective use of screening vegetation. With very little water, small gardens in south China often manage to present landscapes that give a feeling of almost limitless depth. To make ordinary ponds look like lakes, their banks are caused to twist and turn, with many overhanging rocks, spits, inlets, and bays. The banks and revetments usually consist of piled rocks planted over with vegetation to give them a natural appearance.

For the benefit of those who wish to admire the scenery, waterside pavilions are built that cast inverted reflections reminiscent of underwater palaces. From these one can watch the ever-changing reflections of the sky in all its moods and shades at dawn and dusk, in wind, rain, or shine; of racing clouds and skimming swallows; of swaying trees and dancing flowers—the splendors of the real and the mirrored combining in pictures that titillate the imagination. It is the presence of water that has inspired paintings and poetry on such themes as "watching crescent ripples that tell of approaching fish" and "swimming ducks that herald the warming of the rivers in spring."

"Making the small evoke the large" and "economy rather than extravagance of means" are principles commonly applied in classical Chinese garden construction, especially in the treatment of waterscapes.

Stone Lion Fountain in the Imperial Garden, Beijing.

Spits, inlets, and bays are built by piling rocks,
as seen here in Nanjing's Zhan Yuan.

ANIMAL LIFE: BORROWING FROM NATURE

Domesticated animals that have ornamental value are often incorporated in garden scenes as a component of the art of classical garden construction. As early as the Western Zhou period three thousand years ago, deer, cranes, and waterfowl were bred in palace gardens for decorative purposes. Many private gardens of the Ming and Qing dynasties (A.D. 1368–1912) also contained parakeets, peacocks, red-crowned cranes, mandarin ducks, and ornamental fish. Such animals, birds, and fish enhanced the natural effect of landscapes. A brace of deer or cranes raised in a free state in the wooded section of a garden at once created the atmosphere of a peaceful, sparsely inhabited natural environment. And the occasional cries of these beasts and fowl, or even the faint sucking noises made by fish rising to the surface to gape at the setting sun, helped to instill in the viewer mental pictures of wide open spaces and thus heightened the garden's artistic appeal.

Animals such as these, although placed in gardens to enhance the scenery, also have value of their own. Their charming appearance and behavior are a joy to viewers and provide much entertainment.

In the thinking of the classical garden constructors, the chief considerations in the selection of animals for palace or private garden, apart from cleanliness, safety, and convenience in raising, were the needs of the scenery and conformity with traditional ideas of auspiciousness and good luck.

Thus, such popular species as deer, cranes, peacocks, and mandarin ducks, besides being tame, lovable, easy to raise, and adaptable to landscapes, also bore some propitious significance. Deer and cranes meant longevity and everlasting youth; mandarin ducks, which always go about in pairs, signified perfect bliss; peacocks, with their magnificent tails, symbolized riches, honor, and glory. Of course, other species devoid of symbolism were employed purely for the atmosphere they lent to the scene. Examples of these are the chickens, ducks, and geese used to embellish rustic and pastoral landscapes in such gardens as the Dao Xiang Cun (Paddy-Sweet Village) and Xing Hua Cun (Apricot Blossom Village).

Caged birds, such as parakeets, mynahs, and songsters, and goldfish raised in bowls and jars, although less natural than birds and beasts kept in a free state, are nevertheless not lacking in interest as decorative appurtenances in and around halls, residences, and studios. On the principle of "borrowing from nature," Chinese classical gardens also purposely made provision for such seasonal visitors as orioles, swallows, bees, butterflies, cicadas, and crickets, all of which gave life and naturalness to a garden. Gardens in cities, in particular, with their peaceful sanctuaries of trees and vegetation, are able to offer such sights and sounds as bees and butterflies hovering over flowers, swallows darting in and out among the branches of weeping willows, cicadas whirring in the trees, and crickets chirping mournfully by the doorstep. With all these, one easily forgets the noisy, traffic-congested streets on the other side of the garden walls, and it takes but little imagination to picture oneself on a wooded hillside or in some rustic retreat.

Generally speaking, the preferred practice in classical gardens was to raise animals and birds in a free state and use them in the scenery in a natural way. They were seldom put in cages and pens and enployed as independent exhibits as in modern zoos. Admittedly, wild birds and beasts have been raised in captivity since ancient times: the palace gardens of the Western Han period (202 B.C.–A.D. 9) contained such rare imported animals as lions and rhinos; palace parks of the Northern Song period (A.D. 960–1126) also bred various wild beasts whose roars shook the capital city at night and made the imperial park seem like some remote jungle. These were merely novelty ploys on the part of the dynastic rulers, however, and were not normal practice.

POETRY: A GUIDEBOOK TO THE LANDSCAPE

Chinese classical gardens are extraordinarily rich in poetic content, many of them having been created on themes taken directly from poems by famous men of letters. The Jia Jing Ming Qin (Moon Bridge over a Babbling Brook) landscape in the Yuan Ming Yuan Imperial Park, for instance, was constructed in the spirit of Bai Juyi's poem "Twin Brooks with Moon Bridges"; and the Wu Ling Chun Se (Spring Scenes of Wu Ling) landscape took its theme from Tao Yuanming's "Land of Peach Blossoms." The same applies to the small spot scenery and pavilions and verandas in the park. Other examples are the Zhi Chun Ting (Spring-Heralding Pavilion) in the Summer Palace, which—as we said before—was named after the lines of the poet Su Dongpo; the Liu Ting Ge (Keep and Listen Pavilion) in Suzhou's Zhuo Zheng Yuan, which derives its name from the lines by Li Yishan, "Keep the remaining lotus leaves, that I may listen to the sound of rain"; and, in the same garden, the Yuan Xiang Ge (Distant Fragrance Pavilion), so named to evoke the saying, "The delicacy of fragrances increases with the distance," from Zhou Dunyi's *Ai Lian Shuo* (*Dissertation by a Lotus Lover*). Generally speaking, whether the garden constructor takes his themes from existing poems or invents original themes of his own, the principle remains the same: his object is to attain a sense of beauty similar to that of a picture or a poem.

Integration of poetry with the art of garden designing is one of the special achievements of Chinese classical garden construction. Poetry is introduced into garden landscapes in the form of couplets written on boards used to adorn gateways and doors, and poetic quotations are carved on stone tablets or rocks, their artistic appeal augmenting and supplementing the sensory effects produced by the three-dimensional art of garden construction. Much in the way annotations are affixed to Chinese traditional paintings, poetic inscriptions are used in gardens to enrich their artistic content, provide viewers with greater aesthetic enjoyment, and help them understand and appreciate the garden's points

Poetic inscriptions used to enrich the artistic content of the garden and provide visitors with aesthetic enjoyment.

of interest. In this connection the above-mentioned boards and tablets serve as a sort of guidebook. An illustration of this is provided by the linear, three-bay open veranda on the western slope of the Hill of Longevity in the Summer Palace. Quite ordinary in itself, this building was invested with no little interest by the mere addition of a horizontal board with the words, "True Picture of Lake and Mountains." Thanks to this poetically suggestive inscription, the visitor who looks down from the vantage point of the veranda seems to get infinitely more aesthetic enjoyment from the scenery than he would otherwise obtain.

The same principle applies in the exploitation of natural scenic spots. By the simple expedient of having an inscription such as "Green Lotus Peak," "Purple Robe and Golden Belt," "Key to the Mountains and Rivers," "The First Fountain under Heaven," or a few lines inspired by the beauties of nature chiseled onto a rock in the midst of an otherwise pristine landscape, a sense of vivacity and intimacy is infused into the scenery and a rapport established between it and the viewer.

Whether the poetry used in garden construction takes the form of couplets and poems written on horizontal and paired vertical boards and on the walls of buildings, or inscriptions carved on upright stone tablets, steles, rocks, and cliffsides, its treatment conforms with the artistic conception of the garden as a whole. Take, for instance, the various types of horizontal and vertical inscribed boards mentioned above. Their ornamental value derives not only from the artistic calligraphy in which the inscriptions are executed, but also from the shapes of the boards themselves and materials of which they are made. Depending on where and in what sort of milieu they are to be used, they are made of wood or bamboo in the shape of rectangles, plantain leaves, or *ruyi* (S-shaped ornaments, formerly symbols of good luck), and painted or lacquered in different colors. Inscribed rocks and stone tablets also serve as embellishments and spot scenes in landscapes and courtyards.

A stone engraved with inscription in Xi Leng (Seal-Engravers' Club), Hangzhou.

Inscribed couplets in the In-Praise-of-Sincerity
Pavilion in Suzhou's Humble Administrator's
Garden.

Calligraphy by the Empress Dowager Ci Xi of the Qing dynasty, engraved on the rocks in the Summer Palace.

A stone tablet engraved with an inscription by Emperor Qian Long of the Qing dynasty, in Bei Hai Park, Beijing.

Inscribed rocks in Chengde's Bi Shu Shan Zhuang (Imperial Summer Resort).

Such, by and large, are the basic elements that go into the composition of classical Chinese gardens. Now we would like to give a brief account of some of the fundamental principles governing the use of these elements in garden construction.

Garden components—hills, bodies of water, plants, animals, and poetry—are organized into picturesque and poetic scenes; visitors enjoy the scenes as they walk along the paths that lead through them. Thus, the landscape type of garden consists basically of scenery (the contents of which are used for both habitation and entertainment) and paths.

SCENERY: THREE-DIMENSIONAL PICTURES

The art of garden building is similar to painting on canvas or paper in that it frequently employs such principles of compositional arrangement as spacing, distance, light and shade, and coloring. The difference is that while painting is done with inks and pigments on a flat surface, gardens are built on a three-dimensional plan in space. Distance on a painting is expressed by making the objects shown larger or smaller in accordance with the principles of perspective; in a garden distance and depth are produced by actually placing objects closer or farther away.

A garden scene can be viewed either from all sides or by entering it. Thus, in the composition of such a scene, every aspect should be made to please the eye, a feat more complicated than painting scenes on canvas or paper. It is indeed difficult to produce a garden scene that is uniformly ideal when viewed from every angle. So, in practice, emphasis is placed on treatment of the angle from which it is most often seen, to make the aspect it presents from that angle as perfect as possible. The remaining aspects, regarded as subsidiary, get only as much attention as circumstances permit.

Many scenes in a garden are arranged in groups called scenic clusters. These clusters are closely interlinked, one serving as a backdrop or foil for another. For this reason a series of intricate techniques has been evolved for dealing with the relations between scenes. Ancient gardens, private or palatial, were often divided into a number of scene clusters, or scenic areas, each with a practical function, e.g., serving the needs of habitation, everyday occupations, entertainment, sight-seeing. One such cluster or area with a dominant position in scenic space was chosen to be the focal point of the garden's scenic composition. Examples of these are the Fo Xiang Ge cluster in the Summer Palace, the White Dagoba and Shanyin Hall group in Beijing's Bei Hai Park, and facing the Distant Fragrance Pavilion in Suzhou's Zhou Zheng Yuan, the group of wooded hills containing the Xue Xiang Yun Wei (Fragrant Snows and Colorful Clouds Pavilion).

On the scenic areas, some afford free access to neighboring areas, others appear to stand apart, and still others are entirely insulated, so that the visitor passes from one area to another without knowing what to expect until a bend in the path suddenly brings the next scene in sight. In the words of the poet Lu You, "As the path seems to end against a mountain or in a river, a new vista appears of shady willows and bright flowers." This device produces a sense of the unexpected that excites the visitor's curiosity and holds his interest.

PATHS TO THE "PICTURES"

Judged solely by the artistic appeal of their lyrical re-creations of nature, the classical gardens are indeed similar to paintings or pictures. But they differ greatly from the latter in the way they are seen and appreciated. A distance always remains between the

The White Dagoba, Bei Hai Park, Beijing.

A bird's-eye view of Suzhou's Humble Administrator's Garden.

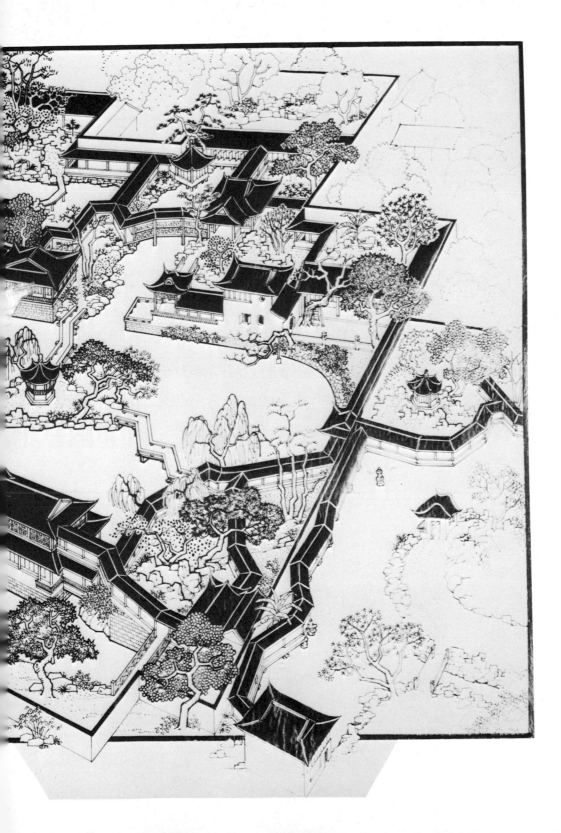

viewer and the picture, and his position in relation to the objects depicted therein is fixed and unchangeable. But a garden must be entered to be appreciated. Thus, it must be furnished with a means by which the viewer can enter its precincts and view its attractions. This medium is the garden path.

The garden path differs in conception from an ordinary path or road. The ordinary road is used to convey traffic—pedestrians and vehicles—and, whether in the form of a city street or a highway through the open countryside, it is constructed on a straight line wherever feasible to make access between one place and another as speedy and convenient as possible. Not so the garden path. Chinese gardens, described as naturalistic and scenic by Westerners, are laid out in natural curves, not in geometric patterns. It would seem that their paths twist and turn about simply to suit the configurations of the hills and lakes constructed in imitation of those in nature. A more ingenious consideration is involved, however. A winding path does not let one see where it leads; it gives subtlety to the scenery, increases its ramifications, creates a sense of seclusion and depth, and prevents the visitor from taking in everything at one glance.

Since a winding path increases the distance between two points, the sightseer's route through the garden is lengthened and the time spent on sight-seeing is increased. As the visitor follows the twists and turns in the path, he is bound to look in every direction. The vistas before him become broader, and an illusion of unlimited depth is cre-

ated in a garden of limited scope. This is the original sense of the popular saying, "A winding path leads to a secluded place," now often taken to mean "Complexity produces a sense of profundity."

The layout of the paths, apart from serving the needs of garden management, is designed chiefly in relation to and for appreciation of the scenery: to provide the ideal angle for looking at a scene or to furnish a line of approach that unfolds the different aspects of a scene to best advantage. In this way, laying out paths is similar to the work of cutting and editing in the film industry. The paths themselves play the role of tourist guides to the sightseer. They lead him through the landscapes and, by the special way in which they are arranged, tell him what to look at, from what angle to look,

A stone archway, Bei Hai Park, Beijing.

Interior of Chang Lang, the Long Corridor.

Winding footpath and bamboo groves inside Suzhou's Ke Yuan.

A small stone bridge.

A stone bridge.

A winding path ascending a rockery hill.

A covered walk.

and whether he is to look as he walks forward or stands in a stationary position.

As it passes through the scenery, a path must cross mountains and rivers and follow the contours of the landscape. In so doing it assumes many different forms: crossing a body of water, it becomes a bridge; going through a man-made hill, it is a tunnel; passing over a hill, it turns into a flight of steps or a zigzagging mountain trail; combined with architecture, it becomes a covered walk or a corridor. These manifold changes provide the land-scape with a good deal of color and interest, and in the best examples of Chinese classical garden construction, paths and scenery are merged into a single entity.

Also seen in gardens are more generally con-ceived pathways in their basic, unaltered form. These are also treated in such a manner as to make them attractive to the eye. Wherever necessary, they are paved in decorative designs that turn the road surfaces themselves into ornamental objects. In the now familiar Summer Palace and in the garden of Suzhou, pathways that lead to halls and pass through courtyards are paved in an extremely attractive manner. On closer inspection it will be seen that the mosaic patterns on them—some rel-atively simple, others as flamboyant as those on silk brocades—are pieced together with pottery bricks, pebbles, slabs of stone, and even such waste ma-terials as broken bricks and tiles and fragments of porcelain and glass. Serving to beautify the envi-ronment as well as to protect the ground surface and prevent it from becoming muddy in rainy weather, these ornamental pavements testify to the ingenuity and inventiveness of the garden-building craftsmen of ancient times.

Ornamental mosaic pavements of this sort are a basic form of pathway in Chinese gardens.

Irregular slates have been used here to build a
pathway that resembles the pattern of broken ice.

4

LOOKING BACK OVER THE PAST THREE THOUSAND YEARS: THE HISTORY AND DEVELOPMENT OF GARDEN BUILDING IN CHINA

Under the blazing sun, swarms of men hurry to and fro like busy ants on a stretch of land ridged with wooded hills, their half-naked torsos streaming with sweat and burned the color of dark bronze. They dig laboriously, pile up earth, surround it with moldboards, and ram it down with heavy wooden tampers.

This scene took place three thousand years ago. King Wen of the Zhou dynasty, who reigned in the tenth century B.C., had ordered a place of amusement built for himself near his capital Gaojing, some thirty-two miles (twenty kilometers) west of today's Changan county, Shaanxi province. Thousands of men were driven to the site to fulfill his wish. Years of back-breaking labor were required to complete the project, and when it was done, a high earthen terrace had been erected, a large pool dug and filled with water, in which fish were raised, and snow-white birds and tame deer

were bred in the surrounding woods. Names were given to these places: the earthen terraces were called Ling Tai (Holy Terrace); the fish pool, Ling Zhao (Holy Pond); and the bird and beast sanctuary, Ling You (Holy Animal Park). King Wen walked around the grounds and was satisfied. Standing on Ling Tai, he could see the distant scenery and the slaves working below; at Ling Zhao he enjoyed the sight of fish swimming in its waters; at Ling You he admired deer and birds wandering about in a free state.

Historical records show that this was probably the first artificial environment built in China purely for the purpose of entertainment. Earlier than that people had never thought of constructing gardens solely for their enjoyment. The legendary Huang Di (Yellow Emperor), who lived during the later stage of the primitive clan society, built a type of garden called *xian pu,* which presumably was used

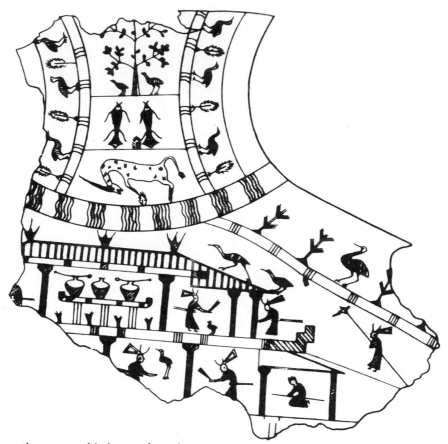

Sketch after a garden engraved in bronze from the Warring States period.

for growing food plants. It is recorded, however, that King Zhou of the Shang dynasty (circa sixteenth through eleventh centuries B.C.) was fond of sight-seeing and hunting. From this one may infer that from the Shang dynasty onward a sort of park designed for hunting and enjoyment had developed from the earlier productive gardens. Such gardens were called *you,* or animal parks. From then on specialized knowledge accumulated as garden construction proceeded apace during succeeding dynasties. Building techniques as well as the conception of the layout were improved and developed.

By the Spring and Autumn period, the 1.5-mile-(2.5-kilometer) long Gu Su Terrace, the Chun Xiao Gong (Palace of Spring Night), and the Tian Chi (Pond of the Heaven) built by Fu Chai, king of the state of Wu, clearly demonstrated the artistic thinking of the garden constructors of this early stage and the fairly high technical level they had attained. The general practice in this period was to erect high platforms in the palace gardens. Platforms or terraces, independent or serving as foundations for palace buildings, no doubt could be used as defenses against enemy attacks and provided better ventilation and protection against dampness; but as far as garden designing was concerned, they served as vantage points from which to contemplate distant scenery and gratified the desire of ancient rulers to stand above their subjects and be closer to heaven.

After the Qin dynasty unified China in 227 B.C., it combined the experience in garden construction of the former six ducal states and further developed the practice of building palatial gardens in natural scenic spots. Knowing that Qin Shi Huang (the first emperor of the Qin dynasty) cherished dreams of becoming immortal and perpetually enjoying a life of luxury, necromancers told him that he would live forever if he kept his whereabouts a secret from ordinary mortals and flitted from one palace building to another like a celestial being. As a result construction began on the Shang Lin Yuan and A Fang Palace—projects of exorbitant proportions. Although unfinished when the Qin dynasty was overthrown in 207 B.C., they epitomized the achievements and thinking of contemporaneous builders of palace gardens. One result of the necromancers' myth-spreading was the desire to live in a fairyland setting of clouds and forests and mysterious mountains, and this in turn became a guiding principle in the creation of palace gardens.

Built on the grounds of the A Fang Palace, which wound along the foot of Li Shan for over 93 miles (150 kilometers), were "a chamber every five steps and a pavilion every ten," linked by 25 miles (40 kilometers) of covered passageways that enabled Emperor Qin Shi Huang to move about in secrecy. A marker was erected on the summit of Zhong Nan Peak to symbolize the entrance to the palace grounds, and a dam was thrown across Fan Chuan River, forming a big man-made lake. These works showed that the craftsmen had already acquired experience in the artistic treatment of natural scenery—they were able to give it a distinct theme by harnessing the grandeur of nature and touching up certain strategic spots. This was a landmark in the development of classical Chinese garden construction: it helped to create a style for building imperial gardens in scenic spots in which architecture was a dominant factor. By the Han dynasty (202 B.C.–A.D. 220), this style had developed still further, and from it grew the practice of building vast gardens in direct imitation of nature or on themes conceived in the mind of man.

Historical records show that the emperors of the Han dynasty often built their palatial gardens on enormous tracts of farmland forcibly enclosed for the purpose. After Emperor Wu had enlarged

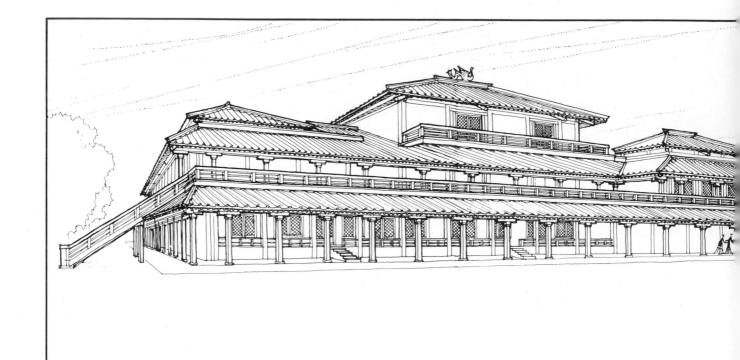

秦咸陽宮第Ⅱ号遺址楊岳原状復図

The Xian Yang Palace built during the Qin dynasty.

the original Shang Lin Yuan of the Qin dynasty, it straddled Changan, Xianning, and three other counties. This practice, of course, seriously impaired agricultural production and brought much suffering to the peasants, but as far as the nascent art of garden construction in China was concerned, it marked an advance of epoch-making significance. The 400 years from the rise of the Han dynasty to its decline saw a tremendous development in garden building. It was then that the foundations were laid for Chinese garden construction as the reproduction of nature by artificial means. Good beginnings were made in such areas as overall conception of gardens, layout for practical purposes, and artistic composition, as well as construction techniques. Concerning the practical function of gardens, for example, new demands were put on garden builders by pleasure-seeking emperors, officials, and rich gentry, which resulted in the incorporation of a series of facilities for such entertainment as hunting, hound running, horse racing, boating, banqueting, admiring fish, birds, and animal life, as well as watching variety shows, and so forth.

The imperial gardens of this period had halls and residential quarters for different seasons of the year. In the imperial garden of Emperor Wu, for example, the Wen Shi Hall (Hall of Warm Rooms) had a room temperature as warm as in spring even in the middle of winter. It was described as having pillars of sweet-scented cassia wood, walls plastered with clay mixed with fragrant spices, wall tapestries of brocade, bed curtains woven of swan feathers,

screens encrusted with pearls and precious stones, and carpets from Ji Bin (an ancient state in the Western Regions). For the summer the Qing Liang Hall (Cool Hall) was furnished with beds and cushions of glazed porcelain, hung with crystal curtains, and festooned with glass icicles, all serving to lower the temperature or at least to give the illusion of coolness.

The fairyland effect sought by earlier creators was carried further by the formation and development of Taoist thinking. This found expression in such garden compositions as "celestial islands in the sea" and "abodes of immortals." The Han dynasty gardens abounded with large, man-made bodies of water, and pond digging and hill construction became the chief props of garden design of that time, as well as of Chinese classical garden building in the succeeding two thousand years. Large bodies of water represented the sea of heaven— the abode of supernatural beings. The Tai Yin Lake situated to the north of the Jian Zhang Palace in Shaanxi province, for instance, symbolized the North Sea in Taoist mythology, and the three islands in it were meant to be the three holy mountains—Penglai, Fangzhang, and Yingzhou. The Jian Tai Terrace in Cang Lake and the Yu Zheng Terrace in Kunming Lake also were inspired by fabled abodes of immortals. Thus, the idealism and utopianism of Taoist beliefs enriched the art of garden building and promoted its development.

The garden builders of the Han dynasty attained a fair amount of proficiency in the use of water. The private garden of Yuan Guanghan, a wealthy man in Shaanxi province, had an artificial sand-and-pebble beach and a swift-flowing river with rocks planted in it to create eddies and whirlpools. That such methods already existed in the second century B.C. is quite remarkable. Another original treatment of water was in the Jian Zhang Palace, where a river was channeled to form a spring. The water was directed through the mouth of a brass dragon, gushed into a cup held by a brass fairy, and then cascaded farther down. Rock hills were another new feature in the landscapes of the Han gardens—a development of the earth mounds of the earlier Qin dynasty. The hills and bodies of water of the Han period were constructed in a naturalistic manner with emphasis on size and grandeur, unlike those of later periods, which were characterized by economy of means.

By the time of the Han dynasty, garden building had already become a composite art form. Statuary was widely employed. Examples of these are the stone figures of the Cowherd and the Girl Weaver, which can still be seen today on the banks of the Kunming Lake, and the 24.5-foot- (7.5-meter) long stone whale in the same body of water; the stone carvings of fish, dragons, and exotic birds and animals in the Tai Yie Lake; and the brass phoenixes that turn in the wind and the brass figures and horses on many palace terraces. Technically speaking, a fair amount of experience had already been gained in hydraulics; in digging, transporting, hoisting, and superimposing masses of earth and stone; in designing and constructing buildings, large and small, singly or serially, against mountains or by the water, cool in summer and warm in winter; in cultivating many different kinds of garden plants; and in raising rare birds and animals, local and imported.

A stone lion sculpture from the Eastern Han dynasty.

During the Three Kingdoms period (A.D. 220–280), garden construction was somewhat hampered by the political division of the nation and the years of uninterrupted warfare that disrupted social production and impoverished the population. But the ruling classes did not give up their pursuit of pleasure and, as historical records show, went on building gardens, one of which was the Tong

Que Tai (Copper Peacock Terrace), built upon the orders of Cao Cao, or Ts'ao Ts'ao, prime minister of one of the Three Kingdoms.

Renewed and bigger developments, however, were registered in garden construction in the period beginning with the State of Wei (one of the states of the Three Kingdoms period), through the Jin dynasty, ending with the Northern and Southern dynasties (A.D. 220–581). During this period a new trend emerged in literature, which expressed the longings of the *literati* and officialdom for a return to nature and secluded living in pastoral surroundings. This trend directly influenced garden construction and helped bring about a new development in landscape design, as did the landscape paintings and literary works extolling nature and the advantages of a life of solitude that appeared during and after the Eastern Jin dynasty. In the period of the Six dynasties, the power and prestige of the *literati* increased and, as they vied with each other in pastoral pleasure-seeking and in keeping up with the new fashions, the gardens of the aristocracy and *literati* in the southern part of China made considerable advances. A quick look at Prince Liang's Tu Yuan (Rabbit Garden) shows that its scenery of hills, lakes, flowerbeds, and bamboo-lined paths was already far superior to the earlier "one pond and three hills" conception of Taoist inspiration. A similar tendency towards the achievement of a pastoral effect was evident in the private gardens of the Northern dynasties. In his "Xiao Yuan Fu" ("Ode to a Little Garden"), Yu Xin of the Northern Zhou dynasty describes it in these words:

Through a scattering of weeping
  willows
And richly green pear and peach
  trees
One sees latticed windows
As he meanders among the lush
  foliage.

In general, the influence of new ideas and the building of large numbers of private gardens during the Northern and Southern dynasties resulted in a new style of garden construction marked by increasingly smaller dimensions and more meticulous layout of the scenery. In areas south of the Changjiang River in particular, this style even affected the palace gardens of the southern dynasties.

Special mention should be made of the rising influence of Buddhism on garden building after the Wei and the Jin periods (A.D. 220–420). The increasingly powerful Buddhist monasteries had by then acquired sufficient social status and financial means to share with emperors, high officials, landlords, and rich merchants the pleasures provided by gardens and parks. By the time of the Northern and Southern dynasties in particular, Buddhist temples in cities all had courtyards and gardens with trees and flowers and even ponds and artificial hills. Monasteries in the countryside often took over and situated themselves on famous mountains and in scenic regions. Thus came the saying: "Most of the famous mountains under Heaven are occupied by

Huang Shan.

Buddhist monks." This practice was not without its merits as far as exploitation of scenic spots was concerned: one should not ignore the role played by Buddhist monasteries and Taoist temples down through the dynasties in the development of such scenic areas as the five holy mountains in north China—Tai Shan in Shandong province, Hua Shan in Shaanxi province, Heng Shan (there are two, both of which are in Henan province and are pronounced the same way in Chinese but written with different characters), and Song Shan—as well as Emei Shan in Sichuan, Lu Shan in Jianxi, Huang Shan in Anhui, and the Mogan and Putuo mountains in Zhejiang province.

By the time of the Sui dynasty (A.D. 589–618), the sumptuous life-style and aesthetic tastes of the ruling classes found expression in the imperial gardens, which displayed an increasing proclivity toward unrestrained luxury and extravagance and an all-inclusive hunt for novelty. The palace gardens of this period abounded with exotic flowers, rare birds and animals, and labyrinthian buildings equipped with mechanical contraptions. In the Xi Yuan (West Garden) of Emperor Yang of the Sui dynasty, flowers and leaves fashioned out of colored silk adorned the bare branches of trees and shrubs in late autumn and winter, and aquatic plants, also made of silk, filled the ponds.

The Tang and Song dynasties (A.D. 618–906; 960–1279) saw another peak period in the development of Chinese classical gardens. The active social life and the advances in literature and art during the Tang dynasty brought new content to the art of garden building. Palace gardens were equipped with well-appointed spas and facilities for sports and games such as horseback polo and *cuqiu* (an early form of football). A new type of garden similar to the public parks in modern cities appeared during this period. Exemplified by the Qu Chi (Winding Pond) in Changan, capital of the Tang dynasty, and the West Lake in Linan, capital of the Song dynasty, they differed from previous gardens in form, use, and methods of management. They were situated within or close to towns and cities and played a prominent part in the everyday life of city residents who flocked to them on festivals and holidays of the Chinese lunar calendar to walk on the grass, admire flowers, go boating, relax in the shade of trees, look at the full moon, climb hills, and watch acrobatics and song-and-dance performances. One could also buy sweetmeats, hairpins, trinkets, toys, and daily necessities in these parks, so that with their hills, lakes, terraces, and pavilions, they were at the same time scenic spots, playgrounds, and marketplaces. In this they very much resembled Beijing's Shi Sha Hai and Jinan's Daming Lake during the more recent Ming and Qing dynasties.

The best scenic spots in cities usually became the sites of Buddhist and Taoist temples or residences and villas belonging to high-ranking officials or rich gentry. Even imperial summer resorts were built at such places, for example, at Qu Jiang (Twisting River) in Changan during the Tang dynasty, at Jin Ming Chi (Bright Gold Pond) in Bianliang (today's Kaifeng) during the Northern

A pond surrounded by rockery, Bei Hai Park, Beijing.

Song dynasty, and at Xi Hu (West Lake) in Linan (Hangzhou) during the Southern Song dynasty. Nevertheless, these places were still open to ordinary people, and their management and exploitation was to some extent in the hands of the local populace. Under the social conditions existing at the time, therefore, much of the scenery took shape spontaneously, along with the development of production. Many bodies of water, for instance, were exploited for growing rice, reeds, and lotus, and for raising ducks, geese, and fish. Thus, in these urban and suburban spots, the arrangement of the architecture reflected, on the whole, the thinking of the native craftsmen and gave rise to a type of scenery done in a simple and natural style. This style, which possessed great vitality, left its imprint on the private gardens of the *literati* and officialdom and even on the gardens of imperial palaces.

Taoism, which flourished during the Tang dynasty, still influenced the art of garden construction. By this time, however, the pond-and-hill composition that originated in Taoist idealism was becoming stylized in the form of an archetype known as the "hill-pond-courtyard." Such courtyard scenes were no longer simple representations of "fairy mountains on the sea"; they were becoming more natural or pastoral in tone and frequently showed distinct signs of having been inspired by poems or paintings. In the Tang dynasty, mountain-and-pond scenes were often attached to large residences and even official mansions, although varying in size and quality of workmanship in proportion to the owners' finances and aesthetic standards as well as the garden designers' accomplishments. Embellishing gardens with *taihu* rocks and rare flowers, as well as raising cranes, had become a regular practice. Private gardens proliferated in the Zhenguan and Kaiyuan periods of the Tang dynasty, and as many as a thousand or more famous gardens could be counted in its eastern capital, Luoyang, alone. During and after the Tang and Song dynasties, the rapid development of landscape painting and of literature describing natural and pastoral scenes gave impetus to the practice of using themes from poems and paintings in garden composition. Meanwhile, direct participation by a growing number of intellectuals and painters in garden building further raised the artistic level of Chinese classical gardens.

Among the palace gardens of the Song dynasty was the famous Fang Lin Jin Yuan (Imperial Park of Fragrant Trees), built in the Zhenghe and Xuanhe periods during the reign of Emperor Hui in the early twelfth century. Here, a rural scene of cottages and rustic inns was created and wildlife raised. And in the early years of the Zhenghe period the Shou Shan Gen Yu (Hill of Longevity Garden) was constructed next to the imperial palace. *Taihu* rocks and rare plants for the hill were transported to the capital from faraway Jiangsu and Zhejiang provinces. This garden, which took six years to create, sported rare and precious plants, tree-shaded walks, flowers that filled the air with fragrance, birds and animals, and a collection of splendid palace buildings.

Private gardens flourished in Luoyang during

the Northern Song dynasty, most of them constructed on the sites of older gardens of the Sui and Tang dynasties. The royal court of the Southern Song dynasty sought ease and comfort in the many gardens it built in the south. The Jin Kingdom in the north took example from the Han people and also built numerous impressive palace gardens.

This magnificent beast, a bronze *hao*, watches over a courtyard in the Imperial Garden in Beijing.

The Yuan, or Mongol, dynasty (1260–1368) inherited the art of building gardens and added to

it certain types of architecture and plant life to which these nomadic people were accustomed. Examples are the An Ying Tai (Hawk-Training Terrace) and the large groves of fontanesia (*Fontanesia fortunei*) in the imperial gardens of the San Hai Zi (Three Seas—the north, central, and south seas) in the Yuan capital of Dadu (today's Beijing).

The gardens of the Ming and Qing dynasties (1368–1912) rose to new heights on the basis of the two-thousand-year tradition of garden construction. The Ming gardens generally contained simple scenery of the open-country type with thatched pavilions, bamboo fences, and trellises as well as buildings of relatively small proportions. Qing gardens, on the other hand, tended toward variegated landscapes with larger buildings and more ornamentation. Ming palace gardens—a good example of which can be seen today in the Imperial Garden in Beijing's Palace Museum—were usually built on the foundations of Yuan imperial gardens. As for the private gardens of the Ming dynasty, many were built in the western suburbs of Beijing noted for their scenic beauty. *Yuan Ye* (*Garden Building*), the only extant treatise devoted entirely to Chinese classical garden construction, was written by a well-known garden designer of the late Ming dynasty named Li Jicheng and is highly rated both in China and abroad.

Many Qing gardens, palatial and private, still exist today. Examples of the palatial variety are the Imperial Garden (called Hou Yuan or Back Garden during the Ming dynasty) in Beijing's Palace Museum, Qian Long Garden, Ci Ning Palace Garden,

Large ornamental rocks in front of a pavilion in
the Imperial Garden (Hou Yuan), Palace Museum,
Beijing.

Above left:
Entrance to the Gulley of Eight Sounds in the hilly sector of Ji Chang Garden in Wuxi.

Above right:
A large rockery in the Imperial Garden, Beijing.

Right:
Large *taihu* rocks are used to form rocky "peaks" in the garden.

御花園

Above left:
Water lilies.

Above right:
Peonies, a symbol of riches
and honor.

Right:
Chrysanthemums.

Opposite:
Trees of precious species are
planted at important points
in the garden.

Right:
An example of the use of water to reproduce a lake in the Humble Administrator's Garden, Suzhou.

Left:
The banks of this pond in the Humble Administrator's Garden, Suzhou, are piled with rocks to give the illusion of a larger body of water.

In the Wang Shi Garden at Suzhou, a small body of water is built to imitate a lake.

A rocky island in Liu Yuan,
Suzhou.

Opposite:
An artificial mountain stream
in Liu Yuan, Suzhou.

"Second Spring in the World"—inscription carved on a horizontal tablet on a wall in Wuxi.

A pavilion in the Imperial Garden of Beijing's
Palace Museum.

Corridor, Bei Hai Park, Beijing.

Part of the Five Dragons Pavilions in Bei Hai Park, Beijing.

Learning-the-Truth Pavilion in the Humble Administrator's Garden at Suzhou.

the Bei Hai Park, Zhong Nan Hai, the Jing Shan Park, the Summer Palace, the Jade Fountain Hill Park, the Fragrant Hill Park in the western suburbs of Beijing, and the Imperial Summer Resort at Chengde in Hebei province. Some of these were damaged during the imperialist invasions of China, but on the whole they retain their original features and dimensions.

Remnants of the private gardens of this period can be seen in some courtyards in Beijing, these being typical of the northern type of garden. In the area south of the lower reaches of the Changjiang River, however, the cream of the garden builders' art will be found. Masterpieces of Chinese classical garden construction are spread throughout the main cities and towns of Jiangsu and Zhejiang provinces. The most representative are those in Suzhou: Huan Xiou Shan Zhuang, Liu Yuan, Zhuo Zheng Yuan, Yi Yuan, Shi Zi Lin, Wang Shi Yuan, Cang Lang Ting, Yi Pu, and others. Garden construction in south China also has its own special styles.

Investigation and reconstruction work is now underway on the sites of some famous historical gardens. Scholars in international academic circles are following this work with interest, since these gardens are examples of China's outstanding cultural heritage as well as of the art of garden building.

Raised ground for planting peonies in Suzhou's Liu Yuan.

Horizontal inscribed board in Suzhou's Wang Shi Yuan.

5

FAR-REACHING INFLUENCE: THE GARDENS OF JAPAN AND WESTERN EUROPE

In the course of three thousand years, Chinese classical garden construction grew into a complete system of garden building that spread to neighboring countries early in history and, during the last two centuries, left its imprint even on gardens in Europe. Its evolution and achievements remain as a brilliant chapter in the world history of garden construction. Basing ourselves on expositions by Japanese and European scholars, we will briefly discuss the influence of Chinese classical garden building on the gardens of Japan and Europe.

INFLUENCE ON
JAPANESE GARDENS

China and Japan have a long history of cultural exchange; the influence of Chinese civilization began to be felt in Japan as long as a thousand years ago. It is, therefore, not surprising that the art of garden building in Japan drew from Chinese classical garden construction during its own formation. Japanese academic circles believe that little garden building was done in their country before the Asuka period (A.D. 593–709). The picture of a domicile engraved on the back of an ancient bronze mirror, found at an archaeological excavation site, shows only a few trees around the building. After the influx of continental culture—with Chinese culture as the main current—during the Asuka and Nara periods (593–793), however, Japanese garden building made considerable headway.

In the late seventh and early eighth centuries (late Asuka period), Taoist thinking and mythology reached Japan, and by the beginning of the ninth century, Japanese builders had adopted the Tang dynasty hill-and-pond theme supposed to represent the abode of the immortals. Gardens of this type became highly popular in the Heian period (794–1185). The pool-and-spring courtyards in the imperial gardens and nobles' residences belonged to this category, while the Toba Rikyu (Birds-Feather Summer Palace) built in 1086 bore a strong resemblance to the Chinese "island of the immortals" garden. This trend in garden construction continued into the Momoyama and Edo periods (1574–1867). The Three Treasure Garden at the Daigo-ji Temple, built in 1589 and acclaimed the *chef d'oeuvre* of the Momoyama period, was constructed on the "one pond and three hills" principle (Penglai, Fangzhang, and Yingzhou). By the Edo period, the "divine islands and holy mountains" theme was widely employed in the building of palatial, monasterial, and private gardens. Later, however, the number of islands was no longer confined to the original three, although the significance remained; anywhere between one and half a dozen might appear in the layout. Further developments on this theme gradually brought forth the typically Japanese "turtle islands" and "crane islands," in a trend that has lasted until recent times.

Another trend in the history of Chinese garden building that affected Japan at the turn of the seventh and eighth centuries was that inspired by Buddhist ideals. In point of fact, Buddhism had an even greater impact on Japanese gardens than it did on those in China. The so-called Maitreya Mountain and the "nine mountains with eight ocean rocks" were both manifestations of this Buddhist influence, which began to find concrete expression in Japanese garden building toward the middle of the Heian period (mid-tenth to mid-eleventh cen-

turies). Another product of this influence was the so-called Jodo (Pure Earth) garden, a typical example of which can be seen at the Moen-ji Temple.

As with Chinese culture as a whole, the art of garden construction was taken to Japan lock, stock, and barrel. Apart from the "holy islands and mountains" and Jodo gardens mentioned above, gardens were built in direct imitation of ancient Chinese creations. One example is the imperial Shinsen-en (Garden of Holy Springs), inspired by the Ling You (Holy Animal Park) of King Wen of the Zhou dynasty. It was one of the palace gardens in the Heian capital, itself built in imitation of the Tang dynasty capital of Changan.

Constantly influenced as they were by Chinese garden-building trends, Japanese gardens also invariably reflected the developments in Chinese social thinking. And although the Buddhist thinking in Chinese garden construction had already affected the gardens of the Heian period, a yet more telling influence was exerted on the thematic content of Japanese gardens by the philosophies of the Chan sect of Buddhism and the neo-Confucianism of the Song dynasty when these philosophies were brought to Japan during the Kamakura period (1186–1333). Adopted by the Buka—the Japanese ruling class at the time—and esteemed and encouraged for political reasons, these philosophies spread so rapidly that, by the Muromachi period (1334–1573), they were deeply rooted among the populace and had become the guiding factors in social conduct. This period also happened to be the golden age of Japanese garden building.

These Japanese bridges and arbors display the influence of Chinese garden structures. (From The American Institute of Architects, *European and Japanese Gardens.* Philadelphia: Henry T. Coates & Co., 1902.)

The influence of the Song and Ming neo-Confucianism is also apparent in the fact that Japanese monks of the Kamakura and Muromachi periods were particularly fond of reciting the lines: "Murmuring streams are like tongues broad and long, and tranquil mountains purify our souls," from a poem written in a naturalistic vein redolent of Chan Buddhism by Su Dongpo, a Song Confucian scholar. At that time Japanese Buddhist monks held a leading position in academic circles, hence Chan (Zen) Buddhism and the neo-Confucian school of thinking became the dominant ideology in Japanese literature and art. This thinking was reflected not only in the manner of composition of Japanese gardens but also in the artistic treatment they received. Examples are everywhere to be seen: in the use of the acoustic properties of pines, bamboo groves, and waterfalls to produce a sense of remoteness and seclusion; in the arrangement of rocky promontories to symbolize Sakyamuni, Guanyin (a Bodhisattva), and Lohans (Arhats); in the carvings of Buddhist figures on cliff faces; in the widespread use of triple-statue combinations, and more.

Frequent comings and goings of diplomats, monks, scholars, and merchants between China and Japan brought a further increase in cultural exchanges; hence, the prompt introduction into Japan of new ideas in Chinese garden building and the love of rustication. For example, when the monk Eisai returned to Japan during the Kamakura period (China's Southern Song dynasty), four years after he had gone to study in China for the second time, he took back Chinese tea and the tea-sipping habit of rustic living. In so doing, he sowed the seed of *chadō* (the tea ceremony) that became the rage in Japan during the Muromachi period (around the middle period of the Ming dynasty) and brought about a revolution in garden construction, one result of which was the emergence of the Japanese *chate* (the garden pavilion or room for tea ceremonies).

Again, when the consummate garden builder Musō Kokushi of the Muromachi period was preparing to build the Tenryu-ji Temple (Temple of the Heavenly Dragon), he engaged in commerce with China to accumulate funds for the project, especially art. The outstanding Japanese painter Setsu Shu's visit to China in 1467–1469 (third to fifth year of the Cheng Hua period of the Ming dynasty) to study painting also gave impetus to the introduction of Ming culture into Japan. Imported landscape paintings of the Song and Ming dynasties in particular had a tremendous effect on the paintings of the Muromachi period. The wash paintings of the Chickabumi school (initiated by Chickabumi Ten and others and based on the style of Ma Yuan and Xia Gui) became highly popular in Japan and established the style for Japan's ink-and-wash landscape paintings.

These developments had a direct bearing on Japanese garden building. In this period Japanese garden builders took inspiration from landscape paintings and even copied their themes straight from the paintings of the Song and Ming dynasties. The influence of the latter could be found in the peaceful and leisurely tone of the gardens and in the practice of constructing multistoried buildings

Although on a much smaller scale than their Chinese counterparts, these Japanese gardens are laid out to imitate the forms of nature in the Chinese tradition. At the top, the *So* style design for a hill garden; at the bottom, the *Shin* style design for a flat garden. (From Tsuyoshi Tamura, *Art of the Landscape Garden in Japan.* Tokyo: Bunka Shinkokai, 1935.)

in them. (As a matter of fact, this practice had already begun in the latter half of the Kamakura period, under the influence of Song graphic art.)

Japanese scholars have observed that the symbolism and abstractionism in Japanese garden-building methods, described as "the condensing of thirty thousand miles into a few feet or inches," should be ascribed chiefly to the importation of Chinese Chan Buddhism and the neo-Confucianism of the Song dynasty. To their influence may be attributed the development in Japanese garden construction of the highly impressionistic "stone courtyard" and "dry landscapes" (or Tang landscapes, in which white sand was used to create the effect of water). Meanwhile, the love for natural and pastoral surroundings evinced by scholars and painters since the Tang and Song dynasties, and especially the naturalism of the neo-Confucianism of the Song and Ming periods—expressed as a creative trend in Chinese garden building—had a far-reaching influence, both directly and indirectly, on Japanese garden building. Also, Japanese rulers of these times thought highly of Song neo-Confucianism and set great store by the Confucian tenet of "going back to the ways of the ancients," which in turn set the tone, at least for the time, for garden construction.

Chinese influence found a more concentrated medium in the person of Zhu Shunshui of the Ming dynasty, a one-time official who was exiled to Japan in 1665 at the death of the Ming dynasty. During the ten or more years before his death there, Zhu was accorded the respected status of teacher by the rulers of that country. When he was not giving lectures, Zhu often engaged in garden building, and his work considerably accelerated the growth of Japanese garden construction. Using techniques from Chinese garden building, Zhu Shunshui revised and touched up the scenery in the famous Koraku-en (Garden of Late Enjoyment), the famous ducal garden in Tokyo so named by Zhu to evoke the quotation, "A man of virtue takes his enjoyment later than others," from *Mencius: King Hui of the State of Wei.* In the pastoral style of south China, he designed and built in the garden a "Full-Moon Bridge"—a stone bridge with a single arch. This was the first time that the Chinese technique of constructing arch bridges was employed in Japan, and it was later imitated by Japanese builders in the execution of the Taikobashi (Rainbow Bridge) in the Shukukei-en (Garden of Condensed Scenery) in Hiroshima in 1781–1788—to give only one of such examples. Other architectural works with Chinese origins in the Koraku-en were: the Seeking Benevolence Hall, dedicated to Bo Yi and Shu Qi and built in accordance with "back to the ancients" thinking of the Confucians; the Little Lu Shan, constructed in imitation of the scenery at China's Lu Shan; and the West Lake Dyke, modeled after the Su Ti and Bai Ti dykes at Hangzhou's West Lake. These "scenes-from-nature" conceptions gained currency and eventually produced a new type of garden—the Daimyo—favored by high-ranking officials and landlords. And the many "mountain scenes" representing Lu Shan in Japanese gardens of this period inspired many other compositions

The Nanzen-ji hojo garden in Kyoto shows the artful use of metaphor for nature. Here a sand garden is carefully raked to give the appearance of waves. (From Tsuyoshi Tamura, *Art of the Landscape Garden in Japan.* Tokyo: Bunka Shinkokai, 1935.)

The use of live animals in a man-made environment may be seen here, with white cranes by the garden lake in Sen-tei, Hiroshima. (From Tsuyoshi Tamura, *Art of the Landscape Garden in Japan.* Tokyo: Bunka Shinkokai, 1935.)

modeled after famous scenic spots in Japan itself.

In the use of plant life, Japanese gardens were influenced by the variegated displays of famous or rare species from China's famous scenic spots for adaptation and cultivation in their own gardens. The first such instance on record is that of the Buddhist monk Ganjin of the Tōshōdai-ji Temple Monastery, who in the Nara period brought pine seeds from China's Gu Shan (Solitary Mountain) at Hangzhou and nurtured them into trees to ornament the monastery garden. This practice became very popular in the Edo period, when many Chinese plant species found their way into Japanese gardens—for instance, the Sichuan willows and West Lake plum trees in the garden of Rikuenkan.

Thus, Japanese garden building was deeply influenced by its Chinese counterpart. Cultural and ideological landmarks in Chinese history that had a bearing on the art of garden construction in China often affected Japanese builders as well—so much so that they even used Chinese legends and folk tales as themes for their gardens. For instance, the Dragon Gate Waterfall, constructed in the Heian period and later developed into a stylized form, had its roots in the Chinese legend "The Silver Carp Leaps over the Dragon Gate." The Tiger Crossing rockery built in the Muromachi period in the garden of the Ryoan-ji Temple took its theme from a Chinese story about migrating tigers crossing a river (see *Book of the Later Han Dynasty: Biography of Liu Kun*). Ancient Chinese accounts concerning the Eight Battle Formations (the fish scale, crane wing, snake, crescent moon, arrow, square, yoke, and flying geese), which reached Japan during the Tang dynasty, inspired the creation of a number of rockeries purporting to represent these formations or versions of them accredited to such Chinese military strategists as Sun Zi, Wu Daozi, and Zhuge Liang. A recent example is the rockery in the Kishiwada Courtyard, built in the 1930s—a group of rocks representing Zhuge Liang's eight battle formations: the commander plus the sky, earth, wind, cloud, dragon, tiger, bird, and snake formations.

Despite the constant assimilation of elements foreign and especially Chinese, the Japanese garden has retained an independent, intact, and characteristic style of its own. On the basis of its traditions, Japanese garden construction has in modern times made remarkable progress, and its high standards, whether in design, building techniques, or management, are acknowledged the world over. China could make use of many of these Japanese standards to modernize her own garden construction, which has fallen behind in recent times.

INFLUENCE ON EUROPEAN GARDENS

Before we discuss the influence of Chinese gardens on gardens in Europe, some other matters pertaining to the subject must be touched upon.

As roads penetrated the regions west of China during the first century A.D., and especially after the "Silk Road" rose to glory during the Tang dynasty, Chinese silks and merchandise streamed

This long walk paved with stone slabs owes much to the Long Corridor (Chang Lang) of the Summer Palace outside Beijing. The English touches include small rock plants in the crevices of the slabs and along the edges beneath the pergola. (From Viscountess Wolseley, *Gardens: Their Form and Design.* New York: Longmans, Green and Co., 1919.)

teenth century saw the beginning of a new stage in Chinese-European relations when communications were reopened in the wake of military expansion by the Mongol Yuan dynasty. In Europe the publication of *The Travels of Marco Polo* in 1298 aroused widespread interest in China and the Orient for the first time. Overland travel between China and Europe was still fraught with difficulties, however; not until the opening of sea routes in the fourteenth century did the obstruction to cultural interflow begin to diminish. Ocean travel and cultural exchanges increased with the growth and expansion of European capitalism. Seafaring was developed by sixteenth-century Portugal, and from the day the first merchant vessel dropped anchor in 1515 at a Chinese port, Chinese porcelains, tea, silks, lacquerware, and handicrafts began to arrive in Europe in bulk. Knowledge about China could also come directly instead of having to pass through many hands and places.

By the seventeenth century, all sorts of stories, factual or fictitious, were being told about China in Europe, which created a desire for all things Chinese. No small number of merchants in Holland, France, and other countries began to manufacture and sell imitation Chinese porcelains, silks, and handicrafts, again enlarging the Chinese influence. Previously, Turkey had epitomized the Orient to European minds, and all things in the decorative arts and handicrafts that had anything oriental about them were called *turquerie.* Now they were being called *chinoiserie* instead. Concrete manifestations of Chinese influence began to appear in

into Europe. For a considerable length of time thereafter, contact with Europe continued, although only intermittently, in the shape of comings and goings of merchants and travelers. Europe, however, knew little at that time about early Chinese society and its cultural achievements. The thir-

France, regarded as the fashion setter in Europe. They were first seen in the decoration in banquet halls and the costumes at masquerades and gradually spread to the decorative arts and handicrafts. This fad owed its inception largely to the ruling classes: Louis XIV was an ardent admirer of chinoiserie and filled his palace with Chinese silks, brocades, porcelains, lacquerware, furniture, and so forth, both real and imitation. Further impetus was given it by the two trade voyages to China by the French merchant ship *Amphitrite* in 1698 and 1703.

The Chinese style of art affected Europe in a manner fundamentally different from the way it influenced Japan and other Eastern neighbors, despite the widespread nature and intensity of the craze for chinoiserie that started in Europe in the seventeenth century and lasted until the early nineteenth century, almost two hundred years. At that time the European nations knew little or nothing about China's history and social conditions, nor did they understand her art. European artists based their judgment and appreciation of things Chinese mainly upon accounts given by merchants and on the mediocre Chinese handicrafts and inferior imitations they saw. Thus the correctness and depth of their judgment, or rather the lack of them, can well be imagined. Not comprehending Chinese art, nor making any serious or conscientious attempt to do so, they interpreted it simply from their own impressions. What Europeans referred to in those days as the "Chinese idiom" stemmed from the Chinese freedom of approach, seen as a strange and novel lack of constraint by Europeans accustomed

Before the Europeans found their passion for chinoiserie, turquerie was the rage. Here is a swan aviary in the Turkish manner and, below it, a second aviary "in the Chinese taste," this one fashioned to resemble a boat. (From *Descriptions Pittoresques de Jardins.* Leipzig: Chez Voss et Co., 1802.)

115

Trade with the Orient inspired such notions, in France and elsewhere in Europe, of scenes from Chinese life. This Sèvres *jardinière* (1761), fanciful though its vision may be, shows recognizable architectural detail from a Chinese garden pavilion. (From The Metropolitan Museum of Art, Gift of R. Thornton Wilson, 1954, in memory of Florence Wilson.)

pean art itself and contained nothing truly Chinese. The development of chinoiserie, according to European scholars, falls into three rather indistinct

Painted wallpaper at the height of the craze for chinoiserie; early 1800s, French, by Arthur et Robert (active 1781–1811). (From The Metropolitan Museum of Art, Rogers Fund, 1922.)

to their own geometrical compositions. It is true that the Chinese objets d'art that found their way into Europe in the form of trade goods did, to a certain degree, give inspiration and substance to the rococo style and contributed to its development. But the many eighteenth-century artists of the rococo school who referred to objects and scenes depicted on Chinese porcelains, textiles, wallpaper, and so forth as they went about their creative endeavors branched off into the bizarre and indulged in a superficial play on effects. Thus we may assume that the so-called chinoiserie that came into vogue in Europe after the seventeenth century was merely the outcome of an intrinsic development in Euro-

and mutually overlapping phases: the so-called unrestrained phase at the turn of the sixteenth and seventeenth centuries when chinoiserie began to replace turquerie, the baroque phase, and finally the imitative phase in artistic creation. More or less the same pattern was to be seen in the development of garden construction.

The Chinese influence on European gardens began to be felt in the second half of the seventeenth century. The Porcelain Trianon built in Versailles in 1670 was in the so-called Chinese idiom. Although neither fish nor fowl and purely imaginative in conception, it nevertheless demonstrated the esteem in which Chinese gardens were held at the time of Louis XIV. On the other hand, the landscape garden in England, which made its advent in the eighteenth century, had mature traditions in that country to fall back upon (although the influence of the natural compositions of contemporaneous chinoiserie was an external factor that should not be overlooked), and no direct or tangible evidence of Chinese influence is to be seen in either the conception or form of the naturalistic pasture-like scenes in the early English gardens.

The publication in 1685 of William Temple's book, *Upon the Garden of Epicurus*, may perhaps be regarded as the first formal introduction of China's garden-building art to European garden designers. The book contained comparative studies and commentaries on the topiary gardens of Europe and the nontopiary Chinese gardens, and in so doing gave impetus to the development of the English landscape style.

William Chambers's *Dissertation on Oriental Gardening*, published in 1772, gave special attention to China's garden construction and strongly recommended that English landscape gardens assimilate points of interest from China's creations. While applauding the achievements of Chinese garden builders, Chambers deplored the crudeness of English garden design and called its landscape style unrefined and primitive. He compared Chinese gardens with those of Lancelot Brown, the famous garden constructor who was then in his heyday, and sharply criticized the pastoral scenes and other works by the Brownian school. Pointing out that Chinese gardens were also modeled upon nature, he ascribed their profundity of conception to the artistic erudition of their builders. Garden building in Europe was still no more than an adjunct of architecture, he wrote, and Brown and others like him were merely vegetable gardeners. Chambers believed that English builders should aspire to greater erudition, and that, in developing their landscape gardens, they should learn as much as they could from China. In earlier years Chambers had visited China as an employee of the Swedish East India Company and during his sojourn had drawn sketches of Chinese buildings, furniture, apparel, etc. In 1757 he published his *Design of Chinese Buildings, Furniture, Dresses, Machines and Utensils,* a book that had a considerable impact on Europe. His *Dissertation on Oriental Gardens,* which came off the press fifteen years later, provided reference material of a more direct nature for the construction of English landscape gardens.

That Chambers's assertions became the subject of controversy in Europe in no way diminished the Chinese influence. On the contrary, this influence kept growing and, contributing as it did to the development of the English landscape garden, eventually produced that offshoot known as the Anglo-Chinese garden. The most famous example of the Chinese or Anglo-Chinese gardens that became the rage in Europe is Kew Gardens in Surrey. In 1758 and 1759, Chambers built a good many Chinese-style buildings in this garden, including the well-known Chinese pagoda.

In France, although signs of Chinese influence had already become apparent in French garden construction in the late seventeenth century, Chinese-style gardens came into vogue only after the English had taken the lead in the eighteenth century. For a time, the Anglo-Chinese garden became the main trend in French garden-building. This trend went to extremes, as exoticism (termed sentimentalism by Western scholars) invaded the pastoral atmosphere of the gardens. What was termed the exotic in French gardens of that period referred mainly to Chinese-style buildings. But under the general heading of Chinese style were included a good many

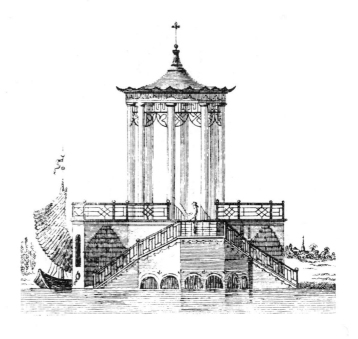

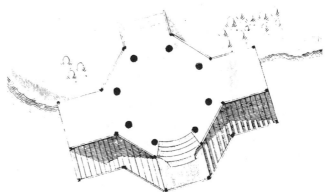

Sir William Chambers's writings on oriental gardening and his works, most notably those at Kew, did more than any other influence to bring Chinese gardens to England. Top to bottom: the Pagoda, the Aviary, and the Menagerie Pavilion, all at Kew. (From William Chambers, *Plans, Elevations, Sections, and Perspective Views of the Gardens and Buildings at Kew in Surrey.* London: 1763.)

This water house for a French garden in the Chinese style provides a platform for fishermen, a mooring for boats, and an eight-columned pavilion atop a double flight of stairs for taking fresh air and viewing the surrounding scene. (From *Descriptions Pittoresques de Jardins.* Leipzig: Chez Voss et Co., 1802.)

Three gondolas in the Chinese style recall the stationary boat-pavilions of the gardens of China. (From *Descriptions Pittoresques de Jardins.* Leipzig: Chez Voss et Co., 1802.)

things that were Japanese, Indian, and Turkish, and later even ancient Egyptian, Greek, or Roman in origin. In fact, as the Anglo-Chinese style entered its late stage, some of the "Chinese-style" architecture in gardens was so elaborated upon by original-minded European garden builders and architects that it became distorted beyond recognition. In form the architectural constructions were vulgar monstrosities done neither in the Chinese tradition nor in that of any other nation. This tendency was most serious in France. According to a count by Eleanor Von Erdberg, there were in France in this period twenty-five well-known gardens that contained architectural constructions done in the so-called Chinese idiom. Few actual examples survive today, but researchers may still find reference to them in many monographs, such as the *Jardins anglo-chinois,* by Le Rouge, published in 1774, the *Description des nouveaux jardins de la France et de ses anciens Châteaux,* by Alexander La Sorde, published in 1809, the *Maisons de compagne,* by Johann Carl Krafft, published in 1876, and *Le Chine en France au XVIII siècle,* by Henri Cordier, 1910.

Thus under the influence of chinoiserie, eighteenth-century French landscape gardening underwent the eclecticism of the Anglo-Chinese style to end up in the pursuit of the baroque and the bizarre, faring less well than its English and German counterparts, which developed in a more healthy manner. The German expert on the history of garden building, H. Jäger, once commented: "The French landscape style, which did not manifest the refined

English taste born of the love of nature, merely imitated the oddities and anomalies from China." Although Jäger's words attested to a questionable comprehension of things Chinese, they nevertheless indicated that landscape gardens in eighteenth-century Europe were, under the influence of the thinking Chinese garden builders, developing along different paths.

Broadly speaking, the Chinese-style gardens and Anglo-Chinese gardens that appeared in Europe merely incorporated certain features culled from superficial impressions of Chinese gardens. The motif of these works was simply a natural landscape; the builders treated terrain, bodies of water, vegetation, and paths so that their contours curved about in a relatively free and easy manner, and they added to the scenery such embellishments as Chinese-style halls, pavilions, bridges, pagodas, and boats. As they imitated Chinese garden types, some even modeled themselves upon local styles in north and south China, as seen in such examples as the so-called Peking-style and Canton-style gardens in Holland. But apart from that, they failed to assimilate the laws and principles of classical Chinese garden construction in all their entirety and profundity.

The landscape garden or naturalistic garden school, on the other hand, developed in a normal fashion under the influence of classical Chinese gardens. Drawing on the experience of the latter and integrating it into their own traditions, works of this type made considerable progress in thematic conception, scenic arrangement, use of plant life,

At the end of an avenue of poplars, this pavilion-capped bridge brings more than a little bit of China to nineteenth-century France. (From *Descriptions Pittoresques de Jardins.* Leipzig: Chez Voss et Co., 1802.)

An English interpretation of a Chinese water garden. (From Viscountess Wolseley, *Gardens: Their Form and Design.* New York: Longmans, Green and Co., 1919.)

A catalog of garden structures that were *la grande vogue* at the end of the eighteenth century: kiosks, pagodas, ruins, painted wooden temples, ten-storied towers, and bridges. (From M. Fouquier and A. Duchene, *Divers Styles de Jardins.* Paris: Emile Paul, editeur, 1914.)

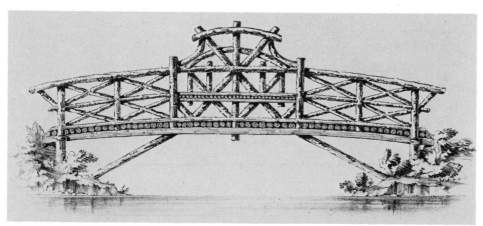

Two rustic bridges, examples of chinoiserie in
England. (From T. J. Ricauti, *Sketches for Rustic
Work*. London: Henry Bohn, 1848.)

design of buildings (which, in these gardens, were proportionately more numerous than in traditional European gardens) and techniques of treatment.

As an example, let us consider the English rock garden. Since the sixteenth century, the English had been domesticating and cultivating mountain plants for the ornamentation of their gardens. At first they simply potted them, but later they planted them in flowerbeds and terraces in the traditional topiary manner. Then, at the close of the seventeenth century, Chinese (and in some instances Japanese) artificial mountains appeared in Europe and produced a host of imitations. These were at first no more than huge and meaningless conglomerations of earth and stone, often with the addition of stiff and awkward caves and small waterfalls. But in the nineteenth century, someone had the ingenious idea of combining them with mountain plants. Creations of this type, after more than one hundred years of practice, summing up, and improvement, finally attained maturity in the 1940s. The famous Rock Garden at Kew was first constructed in 1910 in the way a bricklayer builds a wall. After thirty years of alterations, however, its structure and scenic layout were so much improved and its mountain plants so well combined with rocks and rivulets in the scenery that it has become a fine garden type, structurally complete and highly evocative and original in style. As such it deserves earnest study and emulation by contemporary Chinese garden builders.

A Dutch lath house in the Chinese style. Yew trees were planted against the side of this so-called shadow-house. As the branches grew together and entwined, the appearance was of a green circular house in a wildly overgrown "natural" garden. (From Viscountess Wolseley, *Gardens: Their Form and Design.* New York: Longmans, Green and Co., 1919.)

Since classical gardens are a part of China's cultural heritage, those existing today provide specialists in garden building with much material for research and, moreover, are becoming increasingly popular with sightseers both Chinese and foreign. Visiting a Chinese classical garden gives us the pleasure of studying and beholding the manifold beauties of time and space—a pleasure that visitors from all countries are welcome to share.

INDEX